THE AMAZING BOOK OF

CHESS

LEARN TO PLAY THE WORLD'S MOST POPULAR GAME OF SKILL

GARETH WILLIAMS

CHARTWELL
BOOKS, INC.

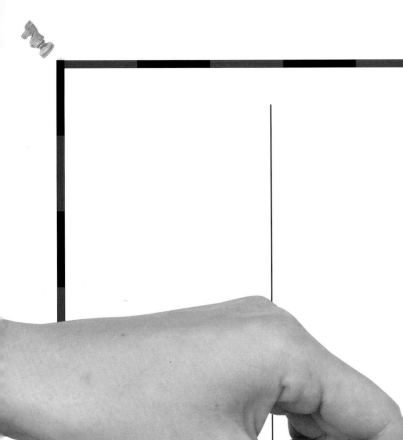

Credits

Photography
Neil Sutherland

Editor
Philip de Ste. Croix

Boardmaker
Neil Hyde

Designer
Stonecastle Graphics Ltd

Photograph Credits
All the historical and archive
photographs in this book are
from the author's own
collection with the exception
of those listed below:
Mark Huba: 115
Hulton Deutsch Collection:
110R, 116T
Popperfoto: 108L, 116B

Production
Ruth Arthur
Sally Connolly
Neil Randles
Karen Staff
Jonathan Tickner

Director of production
Gerald Hughes

Typesetting
SX Composing Ltd, Rayleigh

Color reproduction
Pixel Tech Prepress PTE Ltd,
Singapore

Printed and bound by
Sing Cheong Printing,
Hong Kong

Published by
CHARTWELL BOOKS
a division of Book Sales, Inc.
POST OFFICE BOX 7100
114 Northfield Avenue
Edison, NJ 08818-7100

CLB 4065

© 1995 CLB Publishing,
Woolsack Way, Godalming,
Surrey GU7 1XW,
United Kingdom

ISBN 0-7858-0308-4

THE AUTHOR

Gareth Williams is an experienced chess player who has
captained a number of London teams and was a regular
tournament and county player in the U.K. He is an
established chess teacher: for a number of years he
organized and coached children's classes at his local
primary school.

   He is a regular contributor to the English monthly
magazine *Chess*, writing on the game's history, a subject
on which he is a recognized authority. He is a founder
member of Chess Collectors International and was
elected its Vice President in 1984. With his wife, Vel, he
has been a principal organizer of chess congresses in
London, Paris and St. Petersburg, and was the Exhibits
Co-ordinator for the World Chess Championship match
between Karpov and Kasparov that was held in London
in 1986. He owns one of the finest collections of
historical chess sets in Europe, and pieces and artifacts
from his collection are featured in the book.

INTRODUCTION

Benjamin Franklin (1706-90) was a remarkable man. Famous as a scientist and American statesman, he was also an enthusiastic chess player who wrote the first reference of chess to be published in America. His *"Morals of Chess"* seem as appropriate now, over two hundred years later, as they were when first published in the *Columbian Magazine* in December 1786. This is how he described chess to his public. It is a very positive essay on the benefits of learning to play chess:

"The game of chess is not merely an idle amusement; several very valuable qualities of the mind, useful in the course of human life, are to be acquired and strengthened by it, so as to become ready on all occasions; for life is a kind of Chess, in which we have often points to gain, and competitors or adversaries to contend with, and in which there is a vast variety of good and ill events that are, in some degree, the effect of providence, or the want of it.

"By playing at Chess, then, we may learn:

1st. Foresight, which looks a little into futurity, and considers the consequences that may attend an action: for it is continually occurring to the player. If I move this piece, what will be the advantage or disadvantage of my new situation? What use can my adversary make of it to annoy me? What other moves can I make to support it and to defend myself from his attacks?

2ndly. Circumspection, which surveys the whole Chessboard or scene of action; the relation of the several pieces, and their situations; the dangers they are repeatedly exposed to; the several possibilities of their aiding each other; the probabilities that the adversary make this or that move, and attack this or that piece; and what different means can be used to avoid his stroke, or turn its consequences against him.

3rdly. Caution, not to make our moves too hastily. The habit is best acquired by observing strictly the laws of the game; such as, if you touch a piece, you must move it somewhere; if you set it down, you must let it stand.

"Therefore, it would be the better way to observe these rules, as the game becomes thereby more the image of human life and particularly of war; in which, if you have incautiously put yourself into a bad and dangerous position, you cannot obtain your enemy's leave to withdraw your troops and place them more securely; but you must abide all the consequences of your rashness.

"And lastly, we learn by Chess the habit of not being discouraged by present bad appearances in the state of our affairs; the habit of hoping for a favorable chance, and that of persevering in the search of resources. The game is so full of events, that is such a variety of turns in it, the fortune of it is so sudden to vicissitudes, and one so frequently, after contemplation, discovers the means of extricating one's self from a supposed insurmountable difficulty, that one is encouraged to continue the contest to the last, in hopes of victory from our skill, or at least, from the negligence of our adversary."

Left: Benjamin Franklin's chess set has survived in the keeping of his collateral relatives. This is a typical French playing set of the 18th century, similar to the set with which Franklin would have played during the time he spent living in Paris.

IN THE BEGINNING

The title of this book is very appropriate as chess really is an amazing game. Its beginnings are lost to pre-recorded history. When Alexander the Great invaded India (in about 327 B.C.) and saw for the first time the Indian army of King Porus at Hydaspes, with 50,000 foot soldiers, 1,000 chariots, 130 war elephants and 3,000 horsemen, he was (in a sense) looking at the prototype for chess. Chaturanga, the early Sanskrit name for chess, means "having four limbs" and refers to the four divisions of an Indian army: chariots (rook/castle), cavalry (knight), elephants (bishop) and the foot soldiers (pawns).

THE GAME EVOLVES

Sometime between Alexander's conquest and the 6th century A.D. the game evolved based on these four divisions, but also including a Shah, who had the status of a god and therefore had to be protected at all cost, and a Farzin, counsellor to the Shah. The Arab invasion of Persia brought chess to Baghdad, where in the 9th century as-Suli was known as a great chess master.

The Christian Crusaders loved the game they learned through their Mediterranean battles with the armies of Islam and consequently introduced chess to northern Europe, while the campaigns and conquests of the Moors acquainted Spain and Italy

Left: An exquisite porcelain figurine of a romantic couple playing chess, made in Naples, Italy in around 1800. It was manufactured by the first Capodimonte porcelain company which was licensed by the King of Naples.

Right: Illustrations from William Caxton's *Game and Play of the Chesse*. They show the barbarous King Evilmerodach watching his father being chopped into three hundred piece and fed to the vultures. The philosopher Xerxes (far right) invents chess to explain to the tyrant how he should properly rule over his kingdom.

with the game. By the 12th century chess had firmly established itself as a favorite pastime in the feudal culture of Europe.

During the Middle Ages the game flourished. Although there were slight variations to the rules in different countries, chess was easily recognizable as fundamentally the same game. However, attempts were being made to speed up the play, as the limited movement that the chessmen could make at the time meant development of the two armies was necessarily slow.

At the end of the 15th century a significant change was made to the game. Spanish chess players, experimenting with the moves, enhanced the powers of the queen and bishops, and allowed the pawns an extended move from their initial position. These changes resulted in a faster, more tactical, and thereby more exciting game. The "New Game" was so successful that it spread rapidly throughout Europe, replacing the old rules of chess within an extraordinarily short period of time. The new chess was also known as the Queen's Game.

There is speculation that the extra power and status of this piece was inspired by Spain's Queen Isabella I (1451-1504). She was a very influential woman in her own right, and personally responsible for funding Columbus on his quest to discover the New World. The Italians had another name for the new form: "Mad Queen Chess." Since this time, some five hundred years ago, the rules of the game have remained basically unaltered with no further significant changes.

THE VIRTUES OF CHESS

One of the first books to be printed in England in 1474 was William Caxton's *Game and Play of the Chesse*. Despite the emphatic title, the book has little to do with the playing of chess, being rather a translation from the French of a morality sermon by Jacobus de Cessoles, a Dominican friar who in around 1300 had presented chess as a symbol for morality and stability in society. He believed the game had been invented by a philosopher named Xerxes to teach the tyrant Evilmerodach, King of Babylon, the errors of his ways. Caxton relates the legend in this way:

"In like wise was sometime a King in Babilon named Evilmerodach, a jolly man without justice and so cruel that he had his father's body chopped into three hundred pieces and fed him to the vultures . . .

CHESS IN EARLY LEGENDS

There are a number of myths and legends dating from the earliest Persian literature about the origin of chess. One of the oldest concerns the love of an Empress mother for her two, half-brother, sons, contesting for the vacant throne of the kingdom.

"Half-brothers Gau and Talkhand, as young Princes of a kingdom in North-West India, each considered that his claim to the throne was the stronger. Their widowed mother who acted as regent during their minority loved them both equally. As the years passed their arguments became more bitter, until they eventually came to war with each other.

Left: Caxton's philosopher Xerxes teaches King Evilmerodach the rules of chess, hoping thereby that he will learn tolerance and become a just king. As Caxton puts it, he "showed him how he should amend his ways and become virtuous".

"Under this king Evilmerodach was this game and play of the chess founded. This play found a philosopher named Xerxes, who loveth justice and mercy. And this philosopher was renowned greatly among the Greeks and them of Athens which were good clerics and philosophers. This philosopher was so just and true that he had rather die than to lie and be a false flatterer to the said King. For when he beheld the foul and sinful life of the King, that no man dare blame him. For by his great cruelty he put them to death that displeased him.

"The causes wherefore this play was founded being three. The first was for to correct and reprove the King. For when this King Evilmerodach saw this play and the Barons, Knights, and Gentlemen of his Court play with the philosopher, he marvelled greatly of the beauty and novelty of the play and desired to play against the philosopher. Then the philosopher began to teach him, and showed him how he should amend his ways and become virtuous. The second cause was to keep him from idleness and to keep the people from idleness so that they may prosper. The third cause is that everyman desireth knowledge and study."

Prince Gau, out of respect for his mother's wishes, had given orders that his brother, Talkhand, was not to be killed. Gau's army won the battle, but when his men surrounded Talkhand, the Prince was found to be dead, of fear or exhaustion, but not by battle.

"When the news reached their mother, she became distraught with grief, and accused Gau of murdering his brother. Gau had to find a way to convince her that it was not his doing. He ordered his councillors to recreate the battle in a form that would show his mother how his brother had died. They created the game of chess, showing that when the King was seen they were to shout 'move O King,' and when the King saw his army beaten, and he could not move, he died (was mated) of shame and fatigue.

"Gau took this game of chess to his mother, which explained how Talkhand had died. She studied

it day and night, taking no food or drink until death released her from her sorrow. And from that time chess has remained in the knowledge of mankind."

Similar early legends tell how a philosopher was rewarded for his invention of chess. When the King requested him to state what he wished as a reward, he chose to ask for a quantity of corn. One grain was to be placed on the first square of a checkered board, two grains on the second, four on the third, and so on, doubling up on each following square until the sixty-fourth was reached. The King was impressed by his modest request until he discovered the total amount of corn required to fulfil it: 18, 446, 744, 073, 709, 551, 615 grains would be needed. It has been calculated that this quantity of corn would cover the whole of England to a uniform depth of nearly 38 feet (12 metres)! The King did not know which to admire most – the invention of chess or the ingenuity of the philosopher.

So, as this brief survey reveals, chess has worked its way into the fabric of history and legend. It is one of the oldest established games in existence and we are about to embark on a journey that will reveal more about the history of the board and pieces, and then show you how to master the basic skills of this amazing game.

Left: A German porcelain group showing figures in 18th century costume playing chess. It was probably made in Dresden in the mid-19th century. This was originally a cover for a desk-top ink stand.

Right: This 19th century decorative plate features a painted scene of chess being played in a garden by two ladies in 18th century costume while a young man looks on attentively.

THE BOARD

The board is the battlefield for this game of war. It consists of 64 squares set as eight rows of eight. In their earliest form, game boards were used centuries before the game chess was established. Quite probably they would have been used for chase games played with dice.

THE ASHTAPADA BOARD

The first Indian boards were called "ashtapada," meaning having eight legs. They had markings on some of the squares, indicating that they were designed for games played with counters similar to "ludo." It was the ashtapada board that was taken over and adapted for the earliest form of chess.

The familiar checkered board with which we still play was adopted when the game arrived in Europe in the 11th century. Its design derives from the cloth used in Norman exchequers. This was divided into squares on which the accounts of revenue were kept by means of counters. The boards were larger and heavier in those days and on occasion were even used as weapons. There is a story concerning Prince Henry, the youngest son of William the Conqueror, who became Henry I of England. As a young man, he played chess with Louis, the Dauphin of France. On one occasion, Louis – losing the game – lost his temper, and threw the chessmen at young Henry, while calling him the son of a bastard. Henry, retaliated by picking up the chess board and hit the Dauphin with such force that he would have killed him, if his brother Robert had not pulled him off, and quickly got him away. So, chess has aroused passions from earliest times!

The basic design of the board has not changed significantly since the Middle Ages. On these pages you will find illustrated a variety of boards from different periods and cultures. Although the style of the pieces varies considerably, the look of the boards remains fairly consistent.

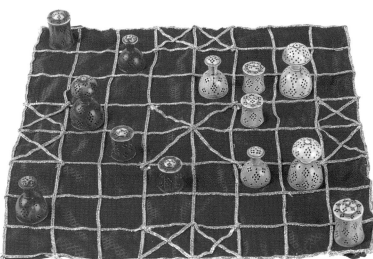

Left: A 17th century Indian Mughal painting of a Hindu god about to play a game on an ashtapada board (similar to that shown above) with a favorite wife.

Above: An Indian silk ashtapada board. The chessmen are 18th century Muslim pieces. They have clappers inside, so that they may be rung like bells.

Below: An Indian board, made in c. 1800, that is constructed of rosewood and inlaid with ivory. The pieces are from a "John" set that was made in Berhampur, Bengal.

Below: A 19th century Indian folding games board made from sandalwood and inlaid with ivory. The chessmen are early 19th century and made of ivory. They were produced for the British, possibly in Visagapatam in India.

Above: A Chinese leather folding board, made in the shape of a large book which contained the elaborately carved ivory pieces. The White king represents King George III, while a Chinese Mandarin leads the opposition.

Above: A Cambodian board made from teak in c. 1820. The horn and ivory chessmen are of a Muslim design that is also found in Thailand.

Left: A scene by Louis Boilly of a chess match at the Café de la Régence, Paris, possibly between Philidor and Legall de Kermuer.

GETTING READY TO PLAY

To place a board ready to start a game of chess there is only one important rule to be observed with regard to the board: *there must always be a white square in the right-hand corner* (**1**).

A simple aide-memoire for the correct disposition of the board is "white on the right." An interesting historical anecdote is attached to this practice. François-André Philidor (1726-1795), who was the strongest chess player of the 18th century, wrote in his *L'Analyze du Jeu des Échecs* in 1748: "The Greeks observed them (rules) strictly, so as not to bear a chess-board wrong turned, having always the idea of a battle before them when they played. They insisted on having the Rook which is on the right hand, placed on a white square, that color being of a good omen among them. And each of the combatants flattered himself by having this white square at his right hand, to obtain the victory."

In keeping with the martial tradition from which chess derives, the squares running from west to east on the board are referred to as ranks (**2**), while the squares going south to north are known as files (**3**). Those crossing the board diagonally are, reasonably enough, called diagonals (**4**). With the exception of the knight, all the pieces move along either ranks, files or diagonals. Now it is time to look in more detail at the individual pieces and the moves that they make.

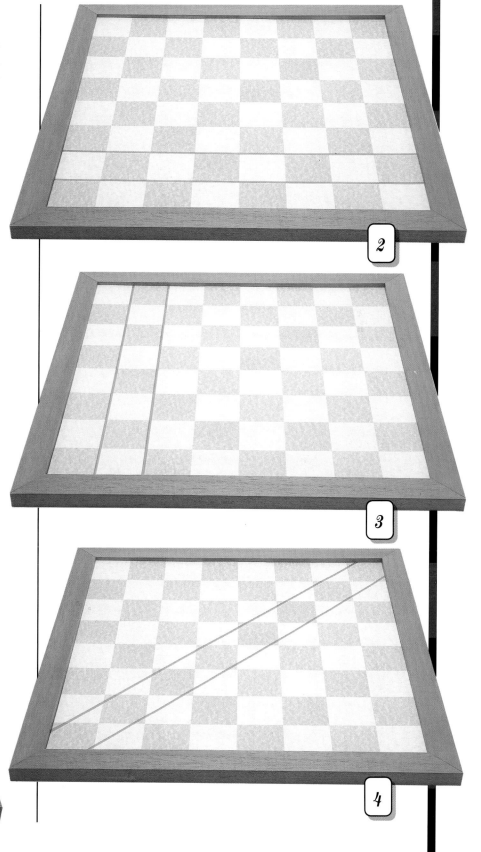

THE CHESSMEN

It is believed that the first chessmen were carved ivory figures that represented the actual named piece. The Shah (king) would be sitting in his howdah on an armored elephant, the knight was a carved soldier riding a horse, etc. In certain countries where carving is an intricate part of the culture, like Burma and Mongolia, chessmen continue to be carved in the form of miniature sculptures. In Islamic countries, the tradition is for abstract design, partly influenced by the Koran's edict which prohibits the worship of images. Christian culture tends to support both decorative and abstract chess sets. Good design in either form will provide visual aesthetic pleasure and excellent equipment for practical play.

THE STAUNTON AND LEWIS SETS

Two good representative sets illustrating the figurative and the abstract styles of design are the Lewis chessmen and the Staunton pieces. Both are pictured here. The Staunton chessmen are the standard pattern of chessmen currently used for all chess tournaments. They are named after Englishman, Howard Staunton, who between 1842 and 1851 was regarded as the world's leading player. The first set made to this design was manufactured by John Jaques and was introduced in 1849. This new design for a chess set was immediately popular due to the clarity of the individual pieces and their stability on the board.

Below: These 12th century Viking pieces, the Lewis men, were found by a farm hand in 1831.

Pawn	Pawn	Rook	Queen	King	Bishop	Knight

Below: The Staunton design is now regarded as the definitive chess set and is used around the world.

Pawn	King	Queen	Bishop	Knight	Rook	Pawn

The Lewis Chessmen are probably the best known of ancient chessmen. They date from the 12th century, and were discovered on the Isle of Lewis off the coast of Scotland in 1831. They represent a medieval Viking army, when even bishops were expected to involve themselves in battles. Visually attractive and well proportioned, the Lewis chess set is a good representation of a decorative set that is also a practical design for playing chess. Two other designs are also illustrated on these pages; they show how variations on a theme lead to beautiful artifacts.

Above: The first "Carton Pierre" casket designed by Joseph L. Williams for J. Jaques & Co. to carry their ivory Staunton pattern chess sets. Staunton (right) was the leading player of his day.

Above: A carved bone set made in Germany in the 18th century. It is seen here in its original container.

Below: A very unusual design made in Austria in the 19th century. The pieces are mounted on spiral stairways.

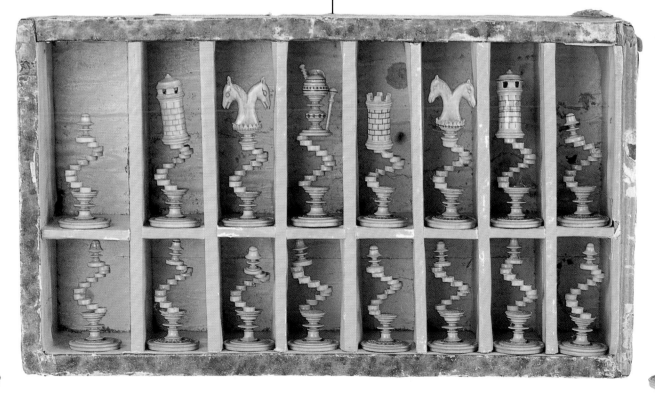

THE STARTING POSITION

To prepare the chessmen for a game, first place a white rook on the white square in the right-hand corner of the board (**1**). Then place the white queen on the central white square (**2**). Two points will help you to remember this: White on the right, and the queen always goes on her own color square. Do this every time the chessmen are placed on the board as it helps correctly to position the remaining pieces.

The king is then placed in the center next to the queen (**3**) and the other rook put on the left-hand corner square (**4**). The bishops are always close to royalty, so place one on either side of the king and queen (**5**). The knights go next to their rooks (or castles) (**6**). Finally a pawn is placed in front of each piece (**7**).

Repeat this procedure on the other side of the board with the opposing chessmen. Black and White should now mirror each other (**8**). You are now in the right position to begin a game.

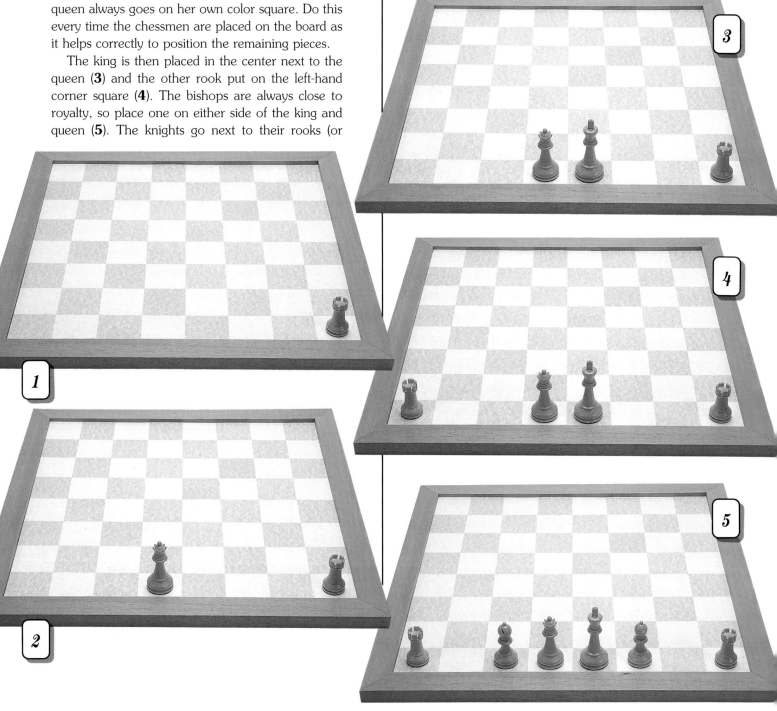

Below: This is how your board should look when you are about to start a game of chess. Note that the bottom right-hand square is white and that the queens are on squares of their own color.

However, before starting it will be helpful to know the relative value of the pieces. A simple method is to use the pawns as the basic unit of "currency." If a pawn is worth one unit, we can reckon the other pieces as follows:

A queen = nine pawns (**9**).
A rook = five pawns (**10**).
Two rooks = ten pawns (**11**).
A bishop = three pawns (**12**).
Two bishops = seven pawns (**13**).
A knight = three pawns (**14**).
Two knights = six pawns (**15**).

THE BASIC RULES

The purpose of the game is to capture the opposing king in a move called **Checkmate**. The technique of how you may capture the king is dealt with in the Endgame section later in the book (see pages 54-65). The first move in the game is always made by White. To choose who plays White, it is traditional for one of the players to hide a white and a black pawn in either hand. The other player points to one hand, and whichever color is revealed in that hand is the color he or she plays in the first game.

Moves are taken in turn, first by White, then by Black. A player is not allowed to miss a turn or make more than one move at a time. Once a piece is touched, it must be moved. A move cannot be taken

back allowing another to be made. With the exception of checkmate, capturing is always done by the attacking chessman moving into the square of an opposing piece and removing it from the board. Capturing is optional: a piece under threat does not have to be taken.

Now we shall look at the individual pieces in turn, learn about their history and development, and how they make their moves in a modern game of chess.

THE QUEEN

"**W**ith rival art and ardour in their mien
At chess they vie to captivate the Queen."

Alexander Pope (1664-1721)

THE HISTORY OF THE PIECE

In the course of chess history Her Majesty has undergone a sex change. She started life on the board as the male confidant of the king, his firzan or wise-man. But when this piece was introduced into England under the unknown name of "fers" and was seen standing next to the king, it was assumed it represented a queen. The English poet Geoffrey Chaucer wrote a poem in 1369, *"The Book of the Duchess,"* to commemorate the death of his friend Blanche, Duchess of Lancaster, comparing the misfortune with the loss of his queen in a game of chess played against Fortune:

"At the ches with me she gan to pleye;
With hir false draughts dyvers
She staal on me, and tok my fers.
And whan I sawgh my fers awaye,

Allas! I kouthe no lenger playe,
But seyde, 'Farewel, swete, ywys,
And farewel al that ever ther ys!'"

The poem is written in Middle English. To paraphrase this passage in modern English: "Then Fortune began to play chess with me. With many deceitful moves, she stole up on me and took my queen. And when I saw my queen taken, alas I could play no longer, but said 'Truly, farewell my sweet, and farewell to everything that is!'."

(i) This queen is believed to represent the French Empress Josephine. It was carved from ivory, circa 1820, in French Indo-China, either for export to Europe or possibly commissioned by a resident French colonist.

(ii) Carved from horn in the 18th century, this is a "Minister" from a Cambodian set. The abstract design conforms with Muslim tradition not to carve images.

(iii) An early 19th century Rajasthan minister, in the same tradition as the earliest Indian chessmen, showing a war elephant carrying cannons into battle, with a tall howdah for the comfort of the dignitaries. The piece is carved from Indian ivory and is lacquered in green and gold.

(iv) A "little faces" chess minister/queen from a Russian set carved in Kholmogory, near Archangel, late 18th century. It is made from walrus ivory and partly stained green.

(v) An early 19th century ivory and ebony queen from Germany. One of the tests of skill to qualify for membership of the German "Guild of Carvers and Turners" was to produce a set in the style of this queen.

(vi) An ivory queen carved in Dieppe, circa 1800. This is in the tradition of French sets made from the 17th century in which carved half-figures were screwed onto turned baluster stems. This style was later copied in northern Europe.

When it represented a wise-man or counsellor in the East, the movement of this chess piece was limited, and similar in scope to that of the king. It could only move one square in a diagonal direction. The firzan's purpose was to remain near the king and to protect him. The design of this chess piece was the same as that of the king, but smaller in size. Initially it was shown as a rider on an elephant, but later it was often represented as a standing figure in the costume of a visier.

When chess came to Europe this piece was called "fers," presumably a corruption of the Persian term "firzan." As early as the 12th century there is a carved ivory queen among the chessmen found on the Isle of Lewis, now displayed at the British Museum. Evidently the metamorphosis from wise-man to queen had occurred by then.

During the 15th century certain changes to the rules of chess were implemented. Christened "New Chess," the changes to the rules are believed to have originated in Spain. One of the most important of the improvements was to enhance the moves of the queen. Her Majesty obtained considerable extra power and a status that revolutionized the battles of the chess board. New Chess spread rapidly through Europe and was so popular that within a short period of time it had supplanted the old rules of play completely. The power of the queen has remained undiminished from that day to this.

HOW THE QUEEN MOVES

The queen is the most powerful piece on the board. It can move any distance along the diagonals, the ranks or the files (**1**). A queen in the center of the board can reach any one of 27 squares if its path is unimpeded. Because of this very power, it is important to be extra careful not to allow it to be taken unnecessarily.

The queen captures by moving into the square of the taken piece. As an example of the queen's power it is illustrated here in a central position simultaneously attacking five pieces and checking the Black king (**2**).

A queen can capture any piece on a square along its run by removing that piece from the board and moving into that square.

Piece under threat

Possible move/ move made

Attacking move

Left: Throughout the book example boards have been annotated with colored arrows and squares to illustrate clearly what is happening. A red square under a piece indicates that it is under threat, and green arrows identify the origin of that threat. Blue arrows show a possible move that a piece can make, or has just made.

1

2

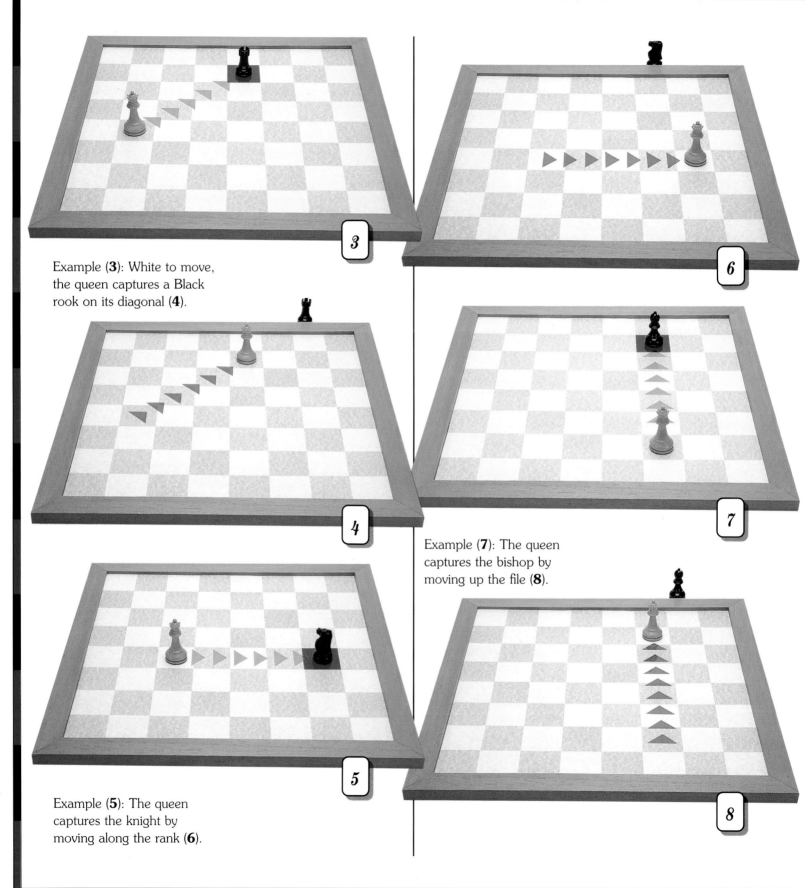

Example (**3**): White to move, the queen captures a Black rook on its diagonal (**4**).

Example (**7**): The queen captures the bishop by moving up the file (**8**).

Example (**5**): The queen captures the knight by moving along the rank (**6**).

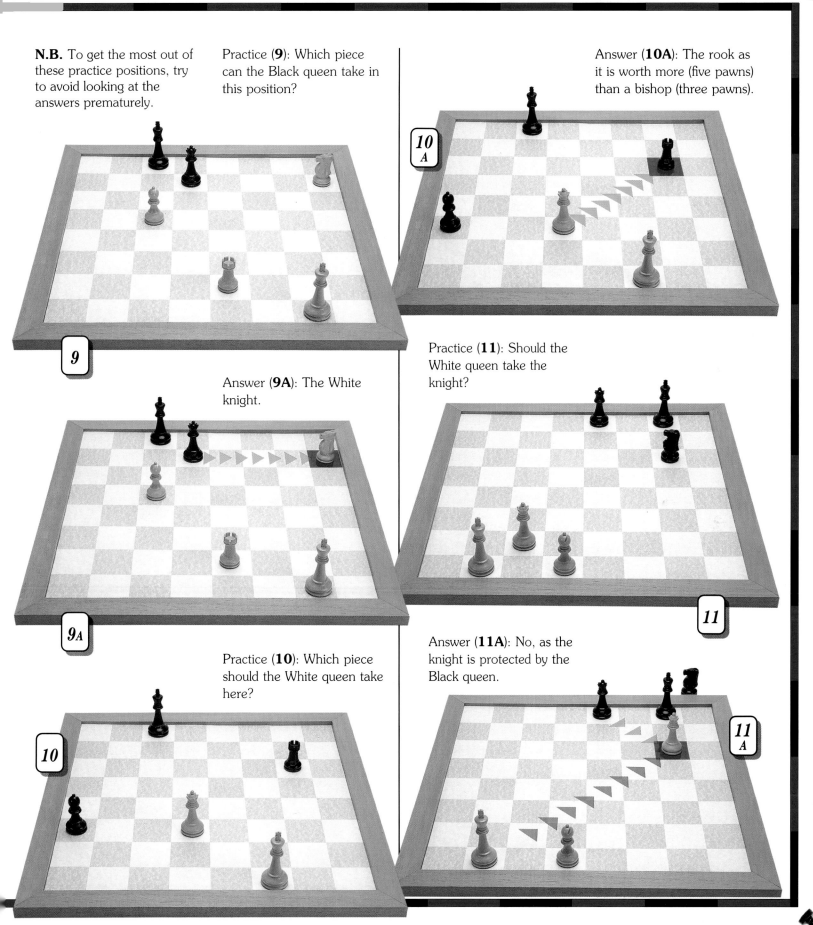

N.B. To get the most out of these practice positions, try to avoid looking at the answers prematurely.

Practice (**9**): Which piece can the Black queen take in this position?

Answer (**10A**): The rook as it is worth more (five pawns) than a bishop (three pawns).

Answer (**9A**): The White knight.

Practice (**11**): Should the White queen take the knight?

Practice (**10**): Which piece should the White queen take here?

Answer (**11A**): No, as the knight is protected by the Black queen.

THE BISHOP

"The third piece of chess, which we call a bishop, the French, fool, the Spaniards, alfarez, and the Italians alfiere segeand, in the East was the shape of an elephant, whose name (fil) it bore."

John Wallis (1616-1703), Savilian Professor at Oxford

THE HISTORY OF THE PIECE

In the ancient game of chaturanga, which was based on the units of the Indian army, this piece was represented by a battle elephant, dressed in armor and ridden by a mahout armed with spears. In Burma and India, the elephant is still the essence of a native chess set. It is possible, in these modern times, to obtain an impressive carved chess set containing eight elephants, four carrying the kings and queens and four ready for battle.

In Arabia the elephant, as a chess piece, was produced in an abstract form, carved like a dome with two small tusk-like protrusions near the top, and called by the Arabic term for an elephant, "al-fil." When the "al-fil" of the chess board came to Europe, where there was no knowledge of elephants, in the Middle Ages, gradually the name was replaced by appropriate alternatives, dependent on the interpretation of differing countries. In England the piece became a bishop, in France a fool, in Germany a messenger, in Italy a standard bearer, and so on. The bishop was another major beneficiary when the rules of the game changed with the introduction of New Chess. Previously it had been a weak piece, only able to jump over one square diagonally. The jump was cancelled, and instead it received the freedom of the diagonal length of the board, greatly extending the range of its influence.

(i) In France the bishop is represented as a "fou" or jester. The carver of this 18th century ivory Dieppe piece has distorted the face and hunched up the shoulder of a priest.
(ii) The oriental bishop was an elephant. In Buddhist Burma this tradition still persists. This beautifully worn 16th/17th century ivory elephant, ridden by a mahout, is typical of Burmese stylized carving.
(iii) In the Austrian Empire, an army officer took the place of the bishop in a chess set. This early 19th century Austrian chess piece, turned and carved from ivory, is an excellent example of craftsmanship.
(iv) A 19th century wooden Austrian officer's hat is placed on top of a spiral stairway in this unusual design. The complete set from king to pawn are precariously placed on top of spiral wooden blocks.
(v) An English ceramic bishop made at Castleford, designed by David Dunderdale, circa 1820. The Castleford Pottery, Yorkshire, flourished between 1795 and 1821.
(vi) An 18th century bone bishop. This design is referred to as "pulpit" but its origin is a mystery. The sets were believed to be Spanish, without any justifiable evidence. Most have been discovered in England. They date from a period when they could possibly have been made by prisoners of war.

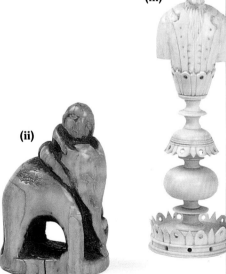

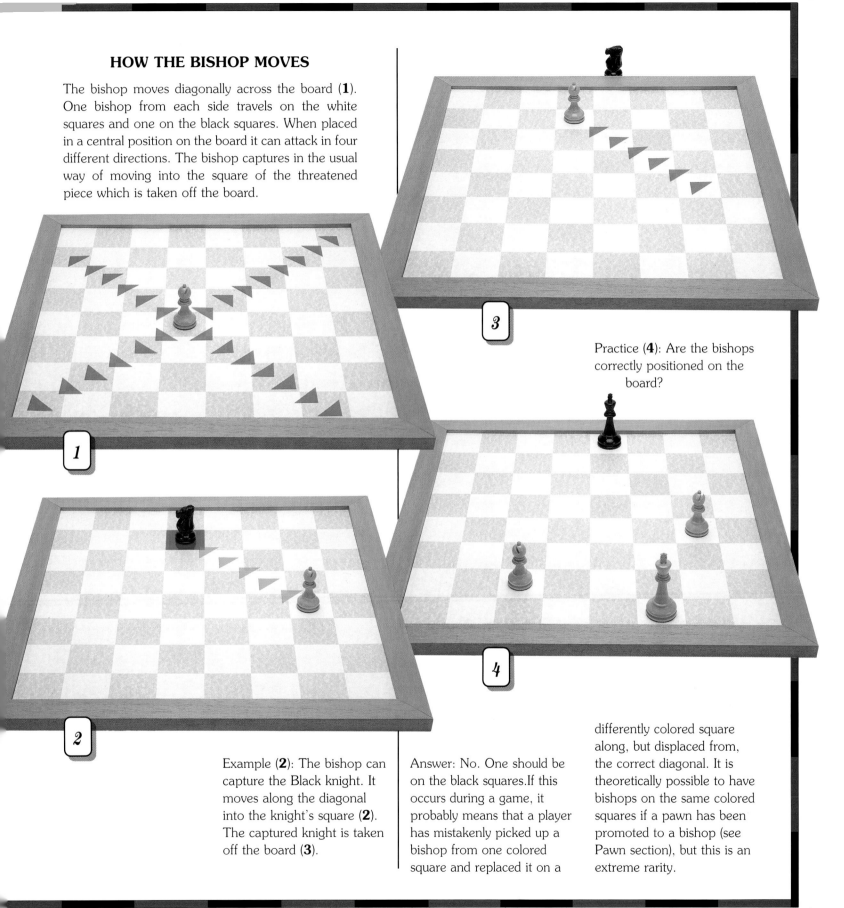

HOW THE BISHOP MOVES

The bishop moves diagonally across the board (**1**). One bishop from each side travels on the white squares and one on the black squares. When placed in a central position on the board it can attack in four different directions. The bishop captures in the usual way of moving into the square of the threatened piece which is taken off the board.

1

3

Practice (**4**): Are the bishops correctly positioned on the board?

2

4

Example (**2**): The bishop can capture the Black knight. It moves along the diagonal into the knight's square (**2**). The captured knight is taken off the board (**3**).

Answer: No. One should be on the black squares. If this occurs during a game, it probably means that a player has mistakenly picked up a bishop from one colored square and replaced it on a

differently colored square along, but displaced from, the correct diagonal. It is theoretically possible to have bishops on the same colored squares if a pawn has been promoted to a bishop (see Pawn section), but this is an extreme rarity.

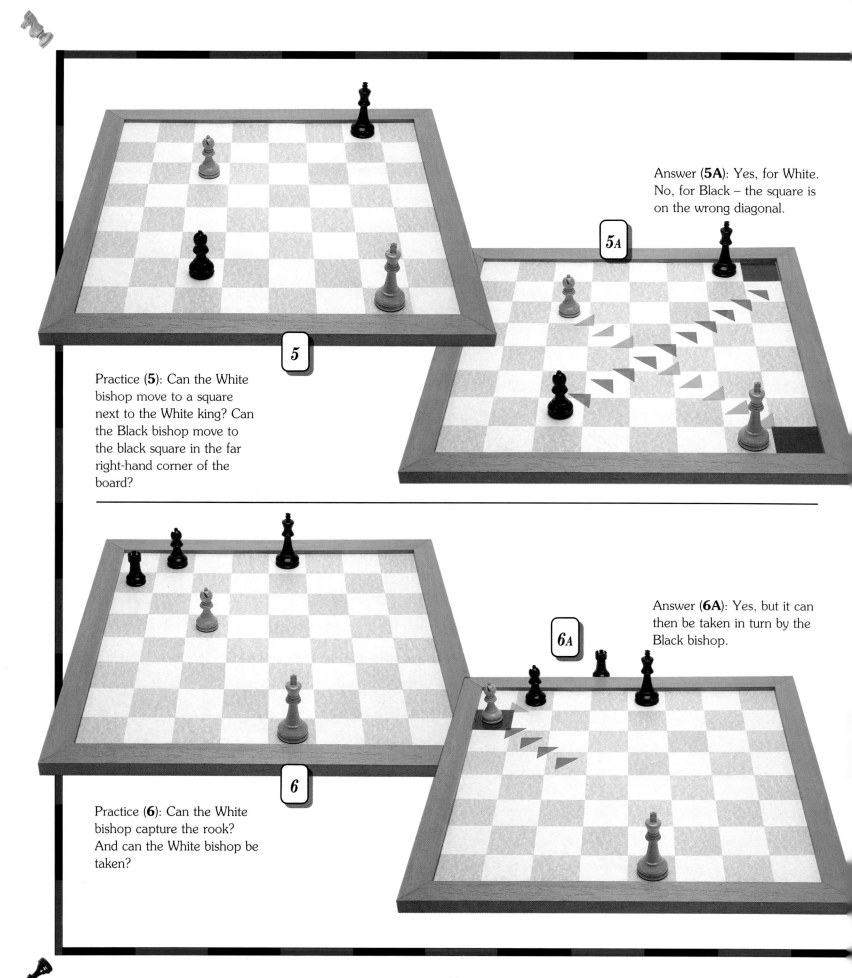

Answer (**5A**): Yes, for White. No, for Black – the square is on the wrong diagonal.

Practice (**5**): Can the White bishop move to a square next to the White king? Can the Black bishop move to the black square in the far right-hand corner of the board?

Answer (**6A**): Yes, but it can then be taken in turn by the Black bishop.

Practice (**6**): Can the White bishop capture the rook? And can the White bishop be taken?

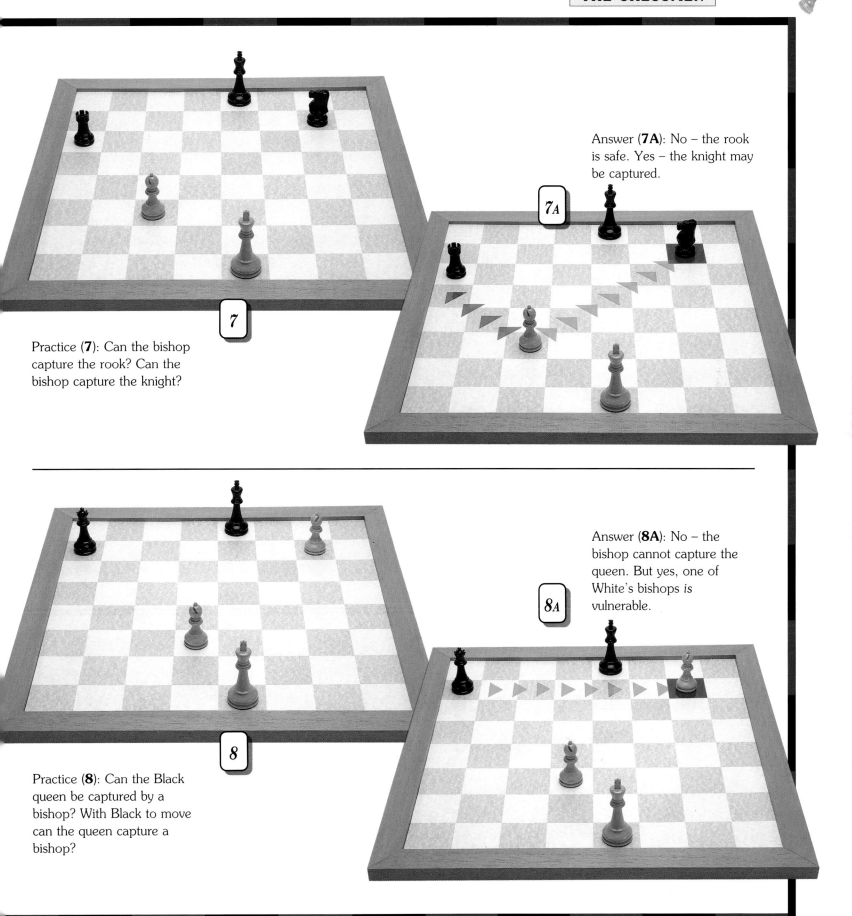

Answer (**7A**): No – the rook is safe. Yes – the knight may be captured.

7A

7

Practice (**7**): Can the bishop capture the rook? Can the bishop capture the knight?

Answer (**8A**): No – the bishop cannot capture the queen. But yes, one of White's bishops *is* vulnerable.

8A

8

Practice (**8**): Can the Black queen be captured by a bishop? With Black to move can the queen capture a bishop?

THE KNIGHT

"Then four bold knights for courage fam'd and speed,
Each knight exapted on a prancing steed:
Their arching course no vulgar limit knows,
Transverse they leap, and aim insidious blows:
Nor friends nor foes their rapid force restrain,
By one quick bound two changing squares they gain:
From varying hues renew the fierce attack
And rush from black to white, from white to black."

Sir William Jones (1746-94), "Caissa: A Poem"

THE HISTORY OF THE PIECE

The knight is the one piece that has undergone no radical change since the game began. The earliest known knight is a chaturanga piece, from a group of 7/8th century A.D. Aphrosiab chessmen. An ivory carving of a rider on a horse, he carries a shield in his left hand and a sword in his right, together with a scabbard and arrows.

By the 9th century the Arabic knight, called "faras," had obtained a simplified symbolic form of a dome with a triangular protrusion to represent a horse's head. This was the shape that became familiar to feudal Christendom. In England the "faras" was eventually renamed "knight," in France, "cavalier," in Germany, "springer," and in Spain, "caballo." By the 14th century the Islamic form of chess knight had been replaced by a carved horse's head. The design for the present Staunton knight was inspired by the rampant stallions that are to be seen on the Elgin marbles, a set of ancient Greek sculptures from the Parthenon in Athens on permanent display at the British Museum in London.

HOW THE KNIGHT MOVES

The knight is the most complex move to learn. It is the only piece that can leap over other chessmen, friend or foe alike. It does a "two-step" – one square forward, or backward, or to the side, then one square diagonally (**1**). If a knight is on a white square it will be covering up to eight black squares and vice versa (**2**).

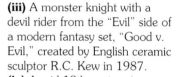

(i) An early 19th century ivory knight – a rearing horse with sword-handling rider. This knight is believed to have originated in French Indo-China. It was made for a European chess set. The native form of chess was played to different rules and with a simple traditional design for the chessmen.

(ii) An early 19th century knight from the Philippines. This exotic design is an omen of good fortune in the local culture. Traditionally it is meant to represent a sea monster that would produce rain and provide protection against fire and lightning.

(iii) A monster knight with a devil rider from the "Evil" side of a modern fantasy set, "Good v. Evil," created by English ceramic sculptor R.C. Kew in 1987.

(iv) A mid-19th century ivory knight, of a design shown in John Jaques & Son's "Pattern Book" 1795 to 1870. Jaques were the major manufacturers of English chess sets in the 19th century. They are still trading.

(v) A 16th century Indian knight, carved from ivory. It is possibly from the province of Vijayanagar. An almost identical one is in the Victoria and Albert Museum, London.

(vi) An Irish knight, from the first part of the 19th century, carved from yew or arbutus wood grown around the lakes of Killarney. The set is part of a box board that could also be used for backgammon.

(i)

(ii)

(iii)

(iv)

(v)

(vi)

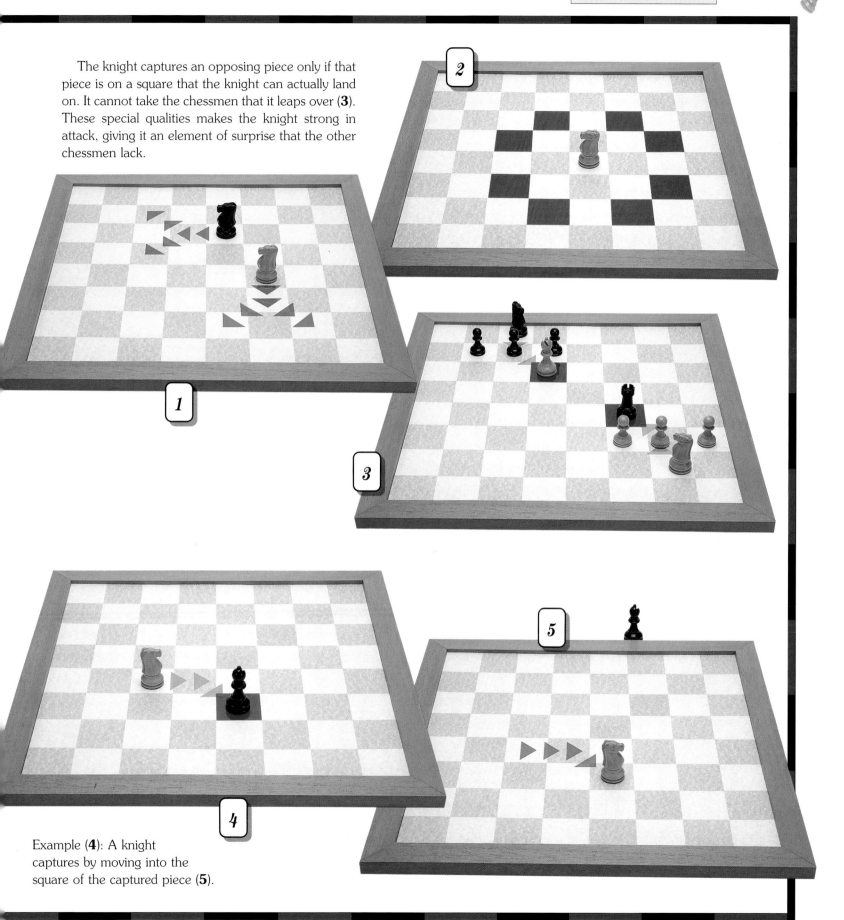

The knight captures an opposing piece only if that piece is on a square that the knight can actually land on. It cannot take the chessmen that it leaps over (**3**). These special qualities makes the knight strong in attack, giving it an element of surprise that the other chessmen lack.

Example (**4**): A knight captures by moving into the square of the captured piece (**5**).

Practice (**6**): Can the knight move to the white square in front of the king? Secondly, can the knight capture the Black rook?

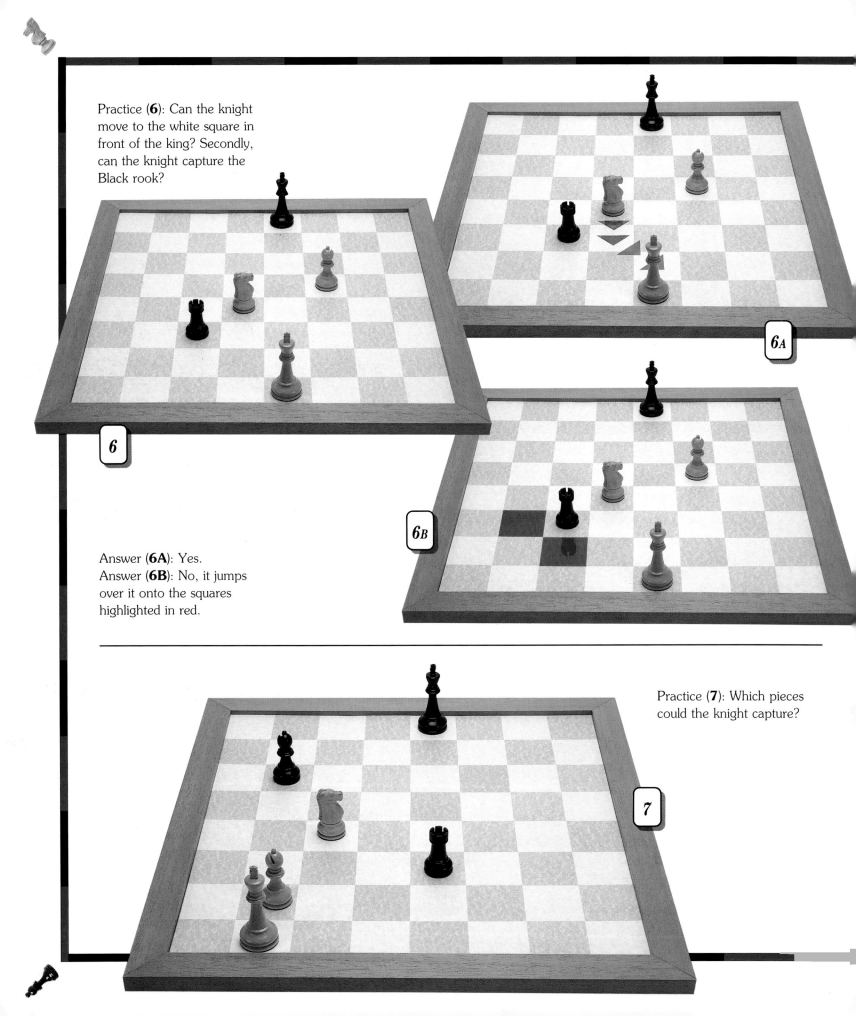

Answer (**6A**): Yes.
Answer (**6B**): No, it jumps over it onto the squares highlighted in red.

Practice (**7**): Which pieces could the knight capture?

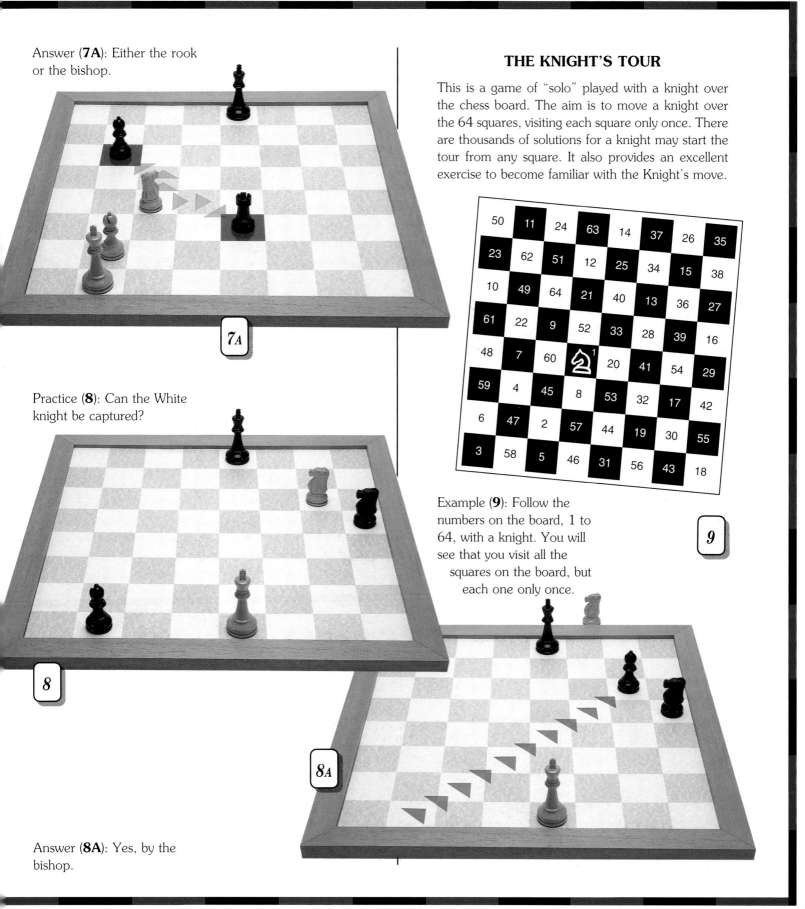

Answer (**7A**): Either the rook or the bishop.

7A

Practice (**8**): Can the White knight be captured?

8

Answer (**8A**): Yes, by the bishop.

8A

THE KNIGHT'S TOUR

This is a game of "solo" played with a knight over the chess board. The aim is to move a knight over the 64 squares, visiting each square only once. There are thousands of solutions for a knight may start the tour from any square. It also provides an excellent exercise to become familiar with the Knight's move.

50	11	24	63	14	37	26	35
23	62	51	12	25	34	15	38
10	49	64	21	40	13	36	27
61	22	9	52	33	28	39	16
48	7	60	1	20	41	54	29
59	4	45	8	53	32	17	42
6	47	2	57	44	19	30	55
3	58	5	46	31	56	43	18

Example (**9**): Follow the numbers on the board, 1 to 64, with a knight. You will see that you visit all the squares on the board, but each one only once.

9

THE ROOK OR CASTLE

"The Rooks are reason on both sides,
Which keepe the corner houses still,
And warily stand to watch their tides,
By secret art to worke their will,
To take sometime a theefe unseene,
Might mischiefe mean to King or Queene."

Nicholas Breton (1542-1626), *The Chess Play* (1593)

THE HISTORY OF THE PIECE

The name Rukh, meaning chariot, is mentioned in "Chatrang Namak," the earliest Persian manuscript to allude to chaturanga (chess), in around the 7th century A.D. It mentions that chaturanga is a war game based on the four divisions of the Indian army, one division being made up of rukhs. Historically, war chariots, as used for ancient battles, had been discarded as a part of the Asian army by the 5th century. This has lead to speculation that as a rukh is included as a piece in chaturanga, that the game itself may have evolved during this period.

In Arabian chess the piece retained the name rukh while the shape of the chess piece took on a symbolic, simplified shape of a rider in a chariot. Surprisingly in Europe only England has maintained the name rook, and even here it is also known as a castle. In France it became a "tour," and in Germany a "turm," both words meaning castle or tower. The origin of this term is interesting. In 1527, Vida, Bishop of Alba, published his "Scacchia Ludus," a marathon poem on a game of chess played between Apollo and Mercury in the presence of the other gods. Here he describes the rooks as warring towers borne on the backs of elephants. These descriptions of the pieces were taken up by the chess players of Western Europe. The elephant and castle thus became the standard chess piece to represent the rook in decorative chess sets. In playing sets, it was reduced to a more practical size, and so became just a castle tower. And that is how the rook turned into the castle.

(i) An elephant and castle, carved in Canton, China, in the early 19th century. These sets were made for export to Europe and America. The Chinese have their own version of chess in which they play on the lines of the board and not the squares. Their chessmen are simple disc-shaped pieces.

(ii) A very early stylized chess piece, supposedly of a chariot, Iranian, Nishapur, early 9th century ivory. This design of rook has been discovered in countries as diverse as Egypt, Spain, Italy, Russia, Germany and England. They date from the 9th to the 14th century.

(iii) An English ivory rook from a 19th century chess set manufactured by the firm of Wm. Lund, Cornhill and Fleet St., London. William and George Lund were ivory carvers and turners to the gentry.

(iv) The rook from an English ceramic Castleford set, circa 1820. It is designed in the European tradition for a figurative chess set of a castle tower carried on the back of an elephant.

(v) An 18th century ivory rook from Denmark. This is an attractive stylized chessman representing a popular design of castle/palace with a tiled roof, such as is seen in Denmark, France and Germany.

(vi) 18th century walrus ivory rook from a Kholmogory chess set. In Russia the rook is represented as a "lada" or boat. Apparently ancient Russian boats were similar to chariots, and to cross the many rivers and waterways the boats would often have wheels attached.

(i)

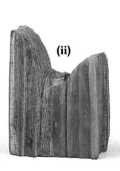

(ii)

(iii)

(iv)

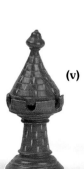

(v)

(vi)

The rook has maintained the same move since the invention of chaturanga. Until the introduction of New Chess in the 15th century, it was the strongest piece on the board. Since then, however, it has had to bow to the power of the newly liberated Queen.

HOW THE ROOK MOVES

The rook, a stronger piece than either the bishop or knight, moves in straight lines along the whole length of the rank and file (**1**). Like the other chessmen it takes by moving into the square of the captured piece and removing it from the board. The rook is the one piece on the board that covers as many squares from a corner of the board as it does in the center. Both rooks illustrated can move to one of 14 available squares.

Example (**2**): The rook captures by moving into the square of the captured piece (**3**).

1

2

3

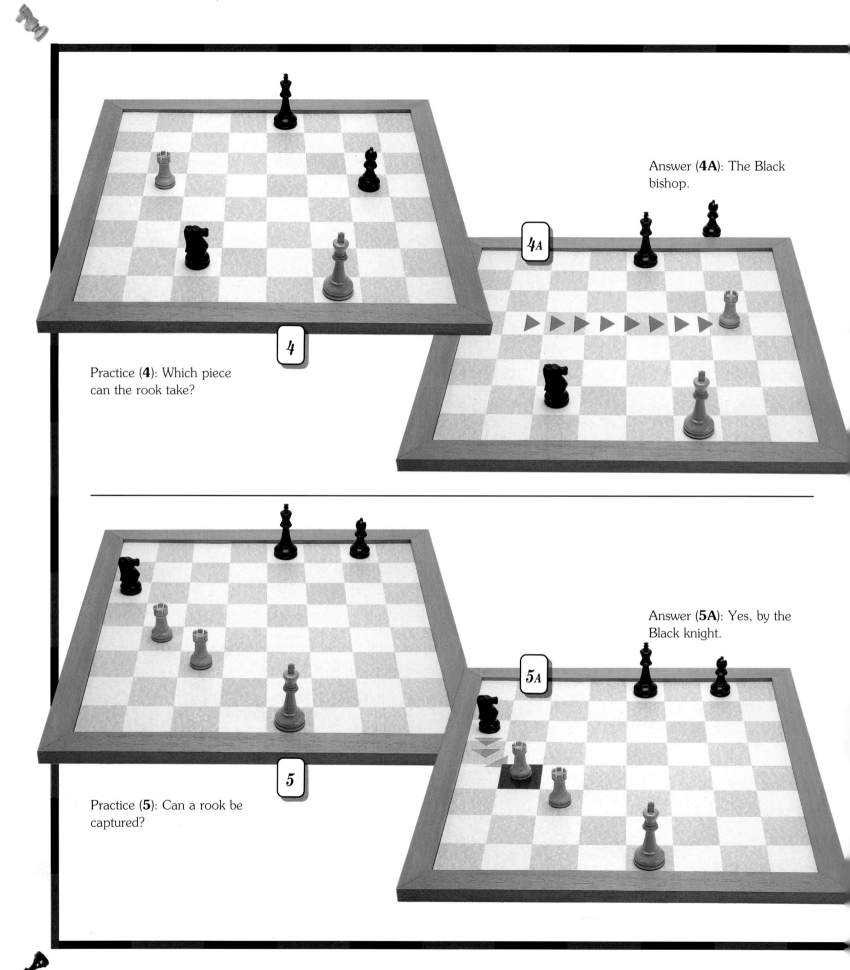

Answer (**4A**): The Black bishop.

Practice (**4**): Which piece can the rook take?

Answer (**5A**): Yes, by the Black knight.

Practice (**5**): Can a rook be captured?

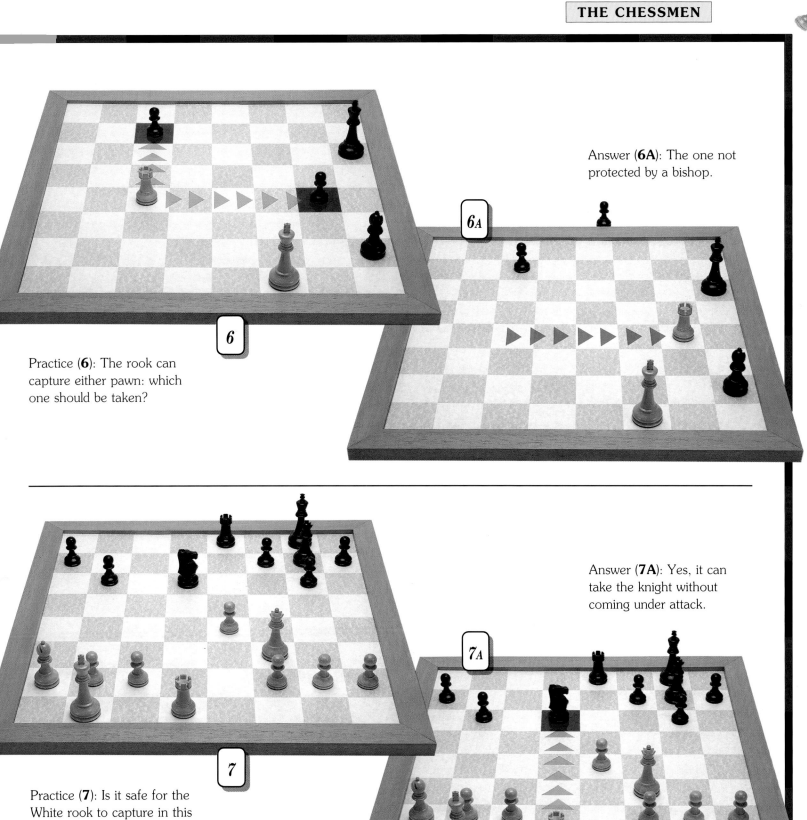

Answer (**6A**): The one not protected by a bishop.

Practice (**6**): The rook can capture either pawn: which one should be taken?

Answer (**7A**): Yes, it can take the knight without coming under attack.

Practice (**7**): Is it safe for the White rook to capture in this position?

THE PAWN

"**M**y chief intention is to recommend myself to the Public, by a novelty no one has thought of, or perhaps ever understood well; I mean how to play the Pawns: *they are the life of this game: they alone form the attack and the defense*; on their good or bad situation depends the gain or loss of each Party."

F-A.D. Philidor (1726-95), chessmaster and composer,
L'Analyze du Jeu des Échecs, 1748

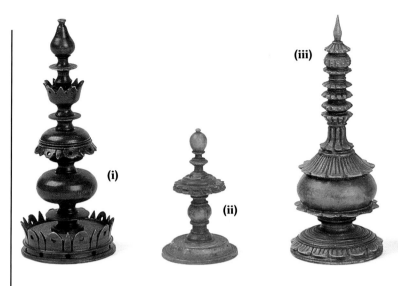

THE HISTORY OF THE PIECE

The pawn has represented foot soldiers throughout the history of the game. Two were excavated in Aphrosiab with the group of 7th century chaturanga figures. These, the earliest pawns to be discovered, are kneeling on their right knees, holding shields in their left hands and short swords in their right. This description could just as aptly apply to pawns carved in India and Burma in the 19th century.

In the Middle Ages, Christian monks tried to identify the pawns as tradesmen, suggesting a different trade for each one. The first pawn was pictured as a farm hand, the second, a smithy, the third, a draper, the fourth, a merchant, the fifth, a physician, the sixth, a taverner, the seventh, a constable, the eighth, a gambler. However, these identities did not generally catch on, and pawns are still associated with the infantry.

Pawns are the weakest units on the board, but their ability to achieve promotion when reaching the last rank of the board endows them with a potential that demands respect.

(i) 18th century Austrian pawn carved, as a peasant, from wood.
(ii) A ceramic caricature pawn, created in 1986 for a comic chess set by Brian Langelean, an English ceramic artist.
(iii) A 19th century ivory carved archer, the figure of a pawn from a carved French set representing the 100 Years War.
(iv) A Chinese soldier from the 19th century. Carved from ivory, stained red, this is a pawn from a chess set to be sold abroad.

(v) Indian Rajasthan flute-playing soldier from an early 19th century chess set. Among the other pawns for this set is a drummer, a flag bearer, some with sword and shield, and the remainder with long native rifles.
(vi) Dating from circa 1800, this is a soldier from the Maharaja's side of a "John" set. The East India Company (the John Co.) had its own private army, which they used to obtain favorable trading terms.

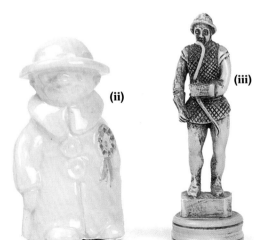

(iv)

(v)

(vi)

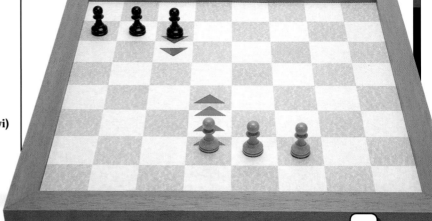

(i) An Austrian 19th century pawn, turned from ivory and stained brown.

(ii) A German 18th century piece, turned from bone and stained red.

(iii) This piece is Indian, 18th/19th century, made of ivory turned on a primitive hand lathe, carved, and stained green.

(iv) This is a French 18th century pawn, made of turned bone and stained brown.

(v) Here we see a Chinese 19th century chessman, turned and carved on primitive hand lathe for export to Europe and America.

(vi) An English 18th century turned ebony pawn.

HOW THE PAWN MOVES

Since the introduction of "New Chess", on its first move each pawn is allowed to choose between moving forward one square or two (**1**). The pawn moves forward along its own file, one square at a time (after the option on the first move). Unlike other pieces the pawn cannot move backwards. When capturing, the pawn changes direction and moves one square diagonally (**2**), taking the captured piece off the board (**3**). It cannot take a piece on the square directly in its path. In this case it cannot move further until the file is clear or it is able to capture an opposition piece by moving diagonally.

PROMOTION

The pawn is the only chessman that can be promoted. When reaching the last rank on the board (**4**), it may be replaced by any other piece except the king. Normally the queen is chosen, this being the strongest piece (**5**). Sometimes, as normally only one chess set is used when playing, the queens may still be on the board when an extra one is needed following a pawn promotion. In such circumstances, a rook turned upside down may be used or the pawn may be marked with a piece of string to designate its new identity (**6**). If no obvious chess piece is available, a button or a coin will do to represent an extra queen until one becomes available.

Practice (**7**): Can the White pawn capture a piece?

Answer (**7A**): Yes – a knight.

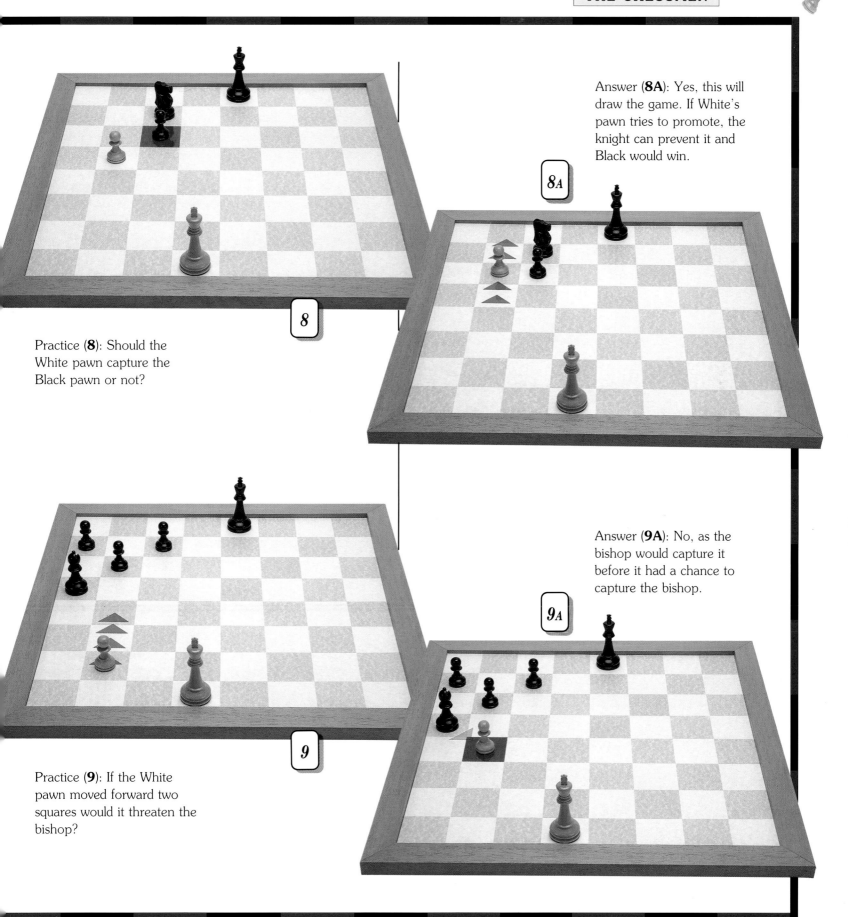

Answer (**8A**): Yes, this will draw the game. If White's pawn tries to promote, the knight can prevent it and Black would win.

Practice (**8**): Should the White pawn capture the Black pawn or not?

Answer (**9A**): No, as the bishop would capture it before it had a chance to capture the bishop.

Practice (**9**): If the White pawn moved forward two squares would it threaten the bishop?

Practice (**10**): This looks similar to (**9**). If the White pawn moved forward two squares would it threaten the bishop?

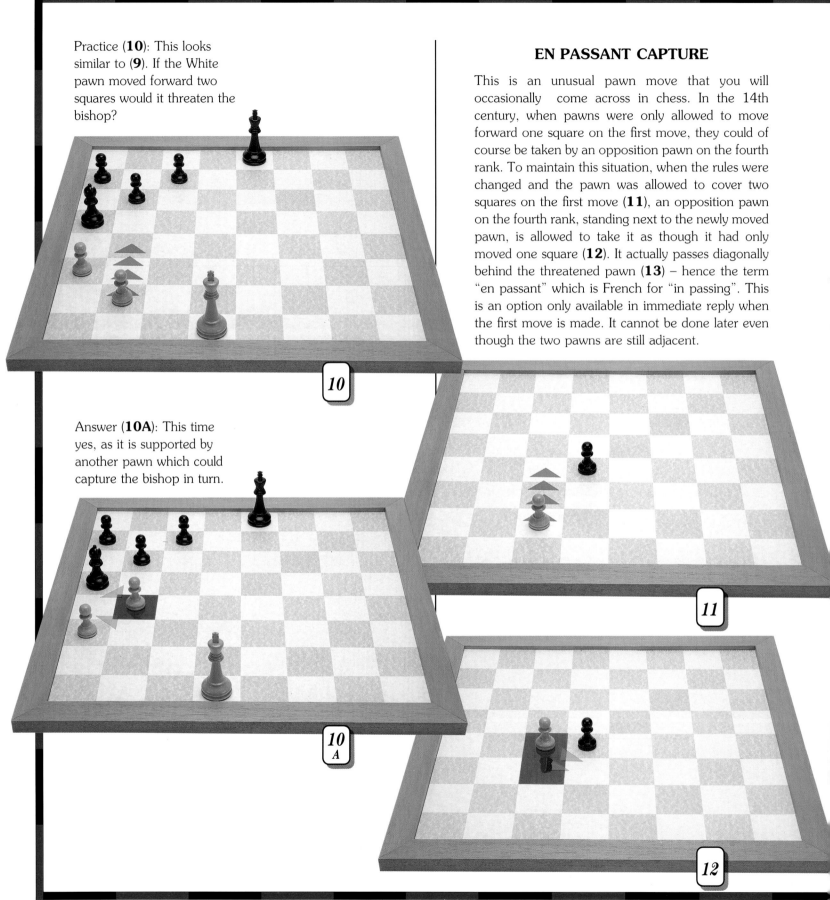

10

EN PASSANT CAPTURE

This is an unusual pawn move that you will occasionally come across in chess. In the 14th century, when pawns were only allowed to move forward one square on the first move, they could of course be taken by an opposition pawn on the fourth rank. To maintain this situation, when the rules were changed and the pawn was allowed to cover two squares on the first move (**11**), an opposition pawn on the fourth rank, standing next to the newly moved pawn, is allowed to take it as though it had only moved one square (**12**). It actually passes diagonally behind the threatened pawn (**13**) – hence the term "en passant" which is French for "in passing". This is an option only available in immediate reply when the first move is made. It cannot be done later even though the two pawns are still adjacent.

Answer (**10A**): This time yes, as it is supported by another pawn which could capture the bishop in turn.

10
A

11

12

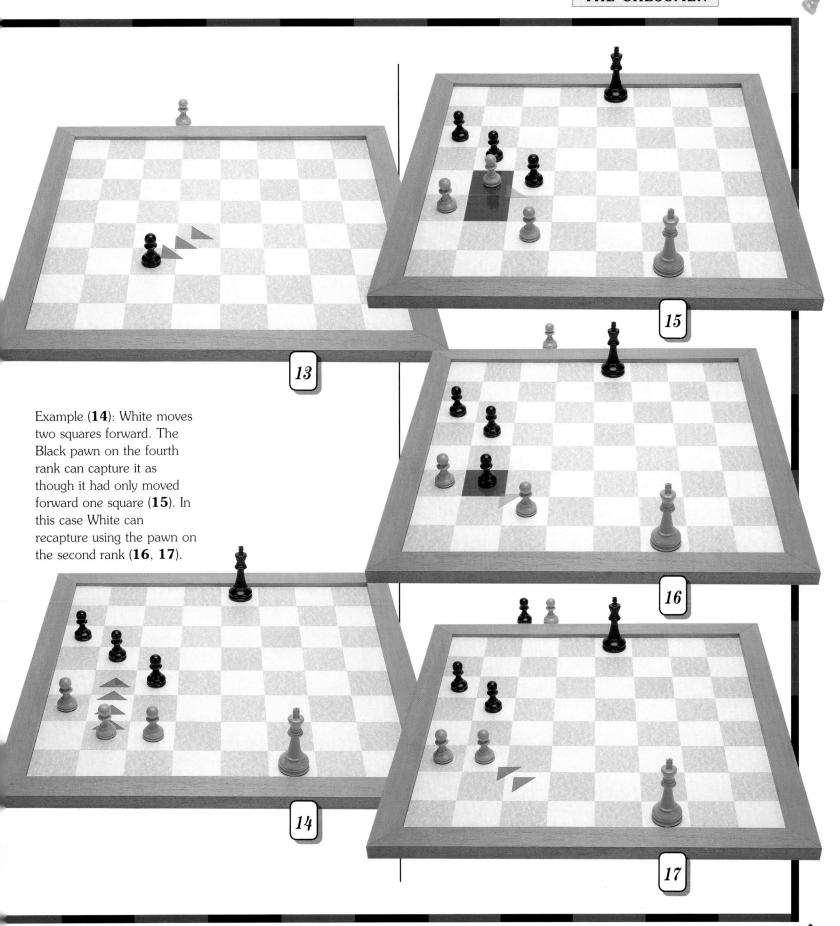

Example (**14**): White moves two squares forward. The Black pawn on the fourth rank can capture it as though it had only moved forward one square (**15**). In this case White can recapture using the pawn on the second rank (**16**, **17**).

43

HOW TO USE YOUR PAWNS

The pawn formation on the board often decides the outcome of the game. There are weak points to be avoided and strengths to be obtained.

Isolated Pawns: A pawn that is on a file that has no support from adjacent pawns is easy prey for the opposing pieces.

Example (**18**): Black has left a number of isolated pawns which will be difficult to defend from White's rooks.

Doubled Pawns: Two pawns of the same color on the same file are difficult to defend and obstructive to attacking ambitions.

Example (**19**): One of the doubled pawns is under attack from two opposing pieces. It has no pawn support of its own to see off the threat. The danger here is that the knight will take the pawn and then move to threaten White's king (**20**). Although the Black knight can be captured, the Black bishop can then capture the rook (**21**). Black has taken a pawn and a rook for the loss of only a knight.

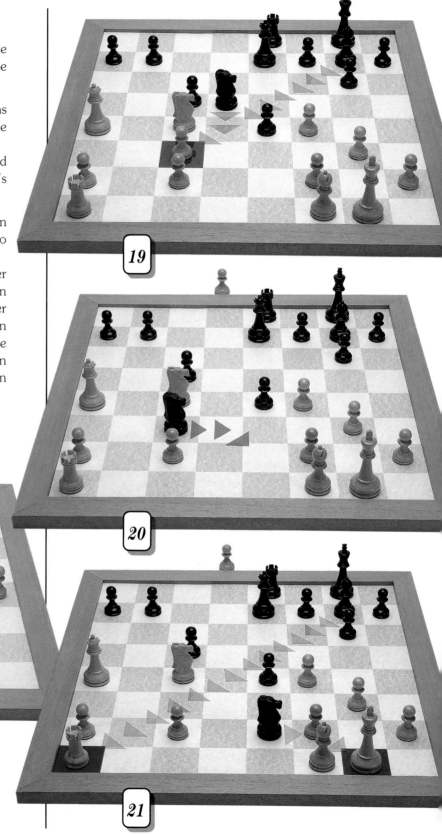

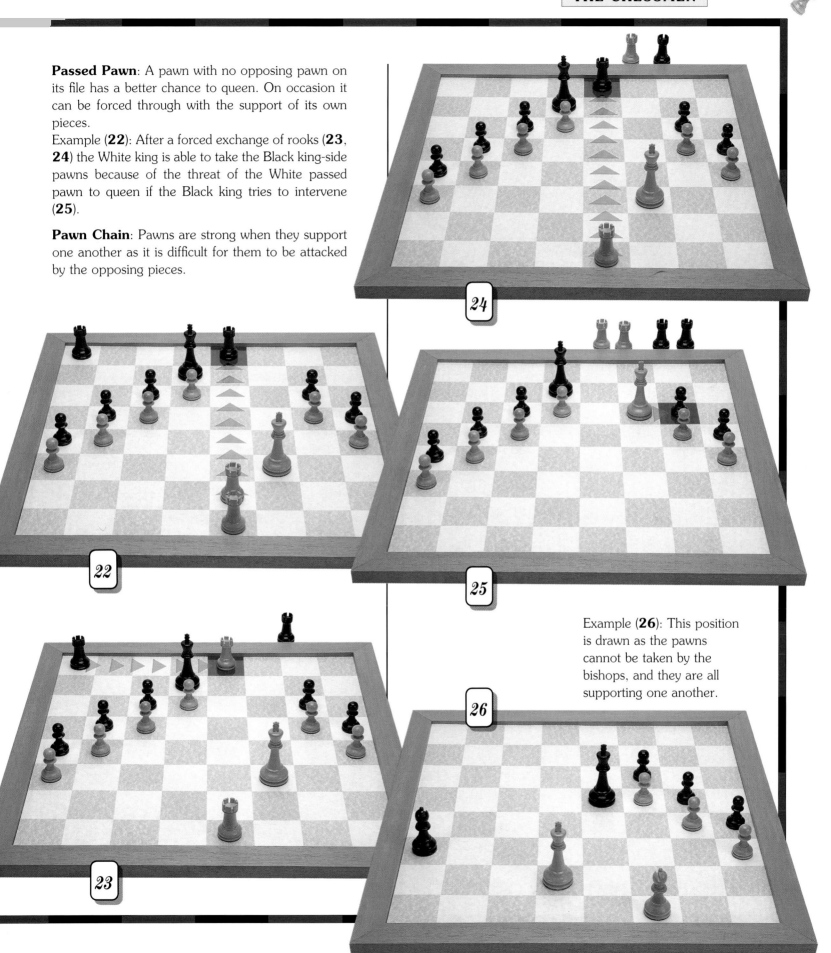

Passed Pawn: A pawn with no opposing pawn on its file has a better chance to queen. On occasion it can be forced through with the support of its own pieces.

Example (**22**): After a forced exchange of rooks (**23**, **24**) the White king is able to take the Black king-side pawns because of the threat of the White passed pawn to queen if the Black king tries to intervene (**25**).

Pawn Chain: Pawns are strong when they support one another as it is difficult for them to be attacked by the opposing pieces.

Example (**26**): This position is drawn as the pawns cannot be taken by the bishops, and they are all supporting one another.

THE KING

"The King must thus be made. For he must sit in a chair clothed in purple, crown on his head, in his right hand a sceptre and in his left hand an apple of gold. For he is the most greatest and highest in dignity above all others and most worthy. And that is signified by the throne. For the glory of the people is the dignity of the King."

William Caxton (1422/91) *Game and Play of the Chesse*, 1474

THE HISTORY OF THE PIECE

The king is paradoxically both the strongest and the weakest of the pieces. He is no feudal king, leading his army into battle, trained as well as any of his knights to gain honor or death in the midst of combat. This is rather an ancient Indian Emperor, a "Shahanshah" or King of Kings, worthy of the utmost respect, to be worshiped and protected. It is his generals who see to war, and fight the battles for the greater glory of the Empire. For, God forbid, if the Shahanshah is captured, all is lost.

This is the king that is on the chess board. Hardly able to defend himself, only being able to move one square at a time, he nevertheless has immense status, as the game can only be won if the king is captured. It is this concept that makes chess such a unique game. It is amazing that this idea, derived from the culture of an ancient civilization some two thousand years ago, has survived unchanged. Since that time, no other intellectual game has been as successful or popular.

As Sir William Jones expressed it in his poem "Caissa" in 1763,

> "High in the midst the reverend Kings appear,
> And o'er the rest their pearly scepters rear:
> One solemn step, majestically slow,
> They gravely move, and shun the dangerous foe:
> If e'er they call, the watchful subjects spring,
> And die with rapture if they save their King.
> On him the glory of the day depends;
> He once imprisoned, all the conflict ends."

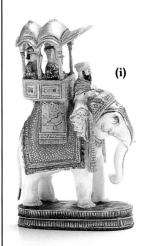

(i) An Indian king, from Murshidbad, 18th century. Carved in ivory with details in red and green polychrome lacquer and gold gilding, it represents a Shahanshah, King of Kings, riding high on a royal howdah, well protected and in an advantageous position to oversee any chess army on the battle-board.
(ii) An ivory carved Danish king, dating from the 17th/18th century. It is from a traditional Danish chess set of a playing design that probably spanned two hundred years.
(iii) An 18th century Russian Kholmogory "Tsar", carved from walrus ivory. The skill of the ivory and bone carvers of Kholmogory was highly respected in Russia in the 17th century.

(iv) A 13th? century king excavated in Milton Keynes, England during the building of the new town. The piece is carved from jet, probably from Whitby, Yorkshire. The design conforms with medieval chess kings; originally the shape represented a king riding in his howdah on an elephant.
(v) A 19th century "Macau" king, carved from ivory. The whole design of the set consists of a conventional plinth with carved heads placed on the pawns and the major pieces.
(vi) An English 19th century king, carved and turned from ivory and stained red. English turners, improving on 18th century designs of chess sets, produced excellent playing sets to the highest quality of craftsmanship.

Originally the chessmen were represented by carved figures of actual rulers. The king would normally be riding in a howdah on a ceremonial elephant. However the earliest excavated king (shah) from Aphrosiab, dating from the 7th/8th centuries A.D., is seen riding in a three-horse chariot, unarmed but carrying a mace, the symbol of his power.

When chess became popular in the Islam civilization a design involving geometric carved chess

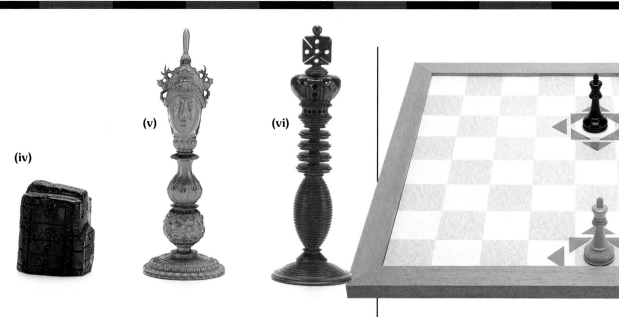

(iv)

(v)

(vi)

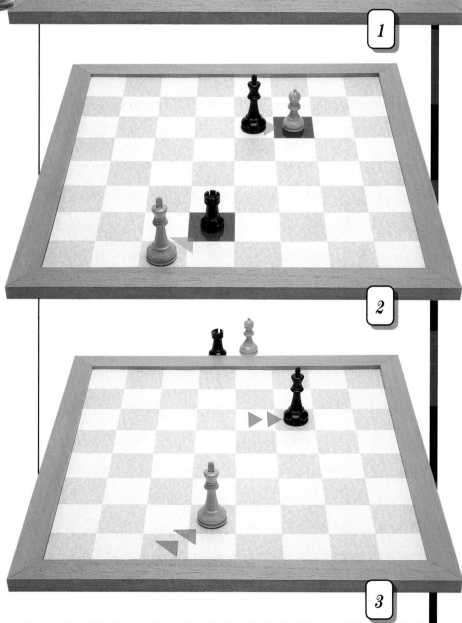

pieces was used. The king would be the largest piece, representing the bulk of an elephant in abstract form, often with a projection from the top to indicate a king in a howdah.

In Europe, from the 14th century, chess sets for play began to be turned in bone, wood and ivory. The pieces obtained an upright appearance, similar to today's conventional sets in which the king is always the tallest piece. Decorative sets were also made, recording contemporary events and the fashions and personalities of the period. The variety of design of chess sets, springing from so many differing cultures and countries and from the imagination of numerous artists and craftsmen, has proved to be virtually as infinite as the moves on the chess board.

HOW THE KING MOVES

The king is the most important piece on the board. A king can never be taken, and when threatened must be warned by the opponent saying "check!" The purpose of the game is to capture the opposing king and when this is achieved, it is checkmate. The end of the game. The word actually derives from the Persian phrase "Shah-mat", meaning "the king is dead". How to achieve checkmate and to win the game is explained in the next chapter.

Kings can only move one square at a time, in any direction (**1**). The king captures by moving into the square of the opposing chessman, which is removed from the board (**2, 3**).

When the king is threatened it must be warned by the attacking player calling "check" and when in "check" (**4**) the king must respond. This can be done in several ways. First, the king can simply move out of the threat. In example (**5**) the king is in check and so moves to an adjacent square (**6**).

Second, the defending player can block the threat by interposing a piece. In example (**7**) the rook breaks the check from the queen by moving into its path (**8**). Third, check can be broken by capturing the attacking chessman. In example (**9**) the knight takes the queen and the king is out of check (**10**). As the king must never move into check, kings can never take one another or even stand next to one another as they would be illegally checking themselves.

6

4

7

5

8

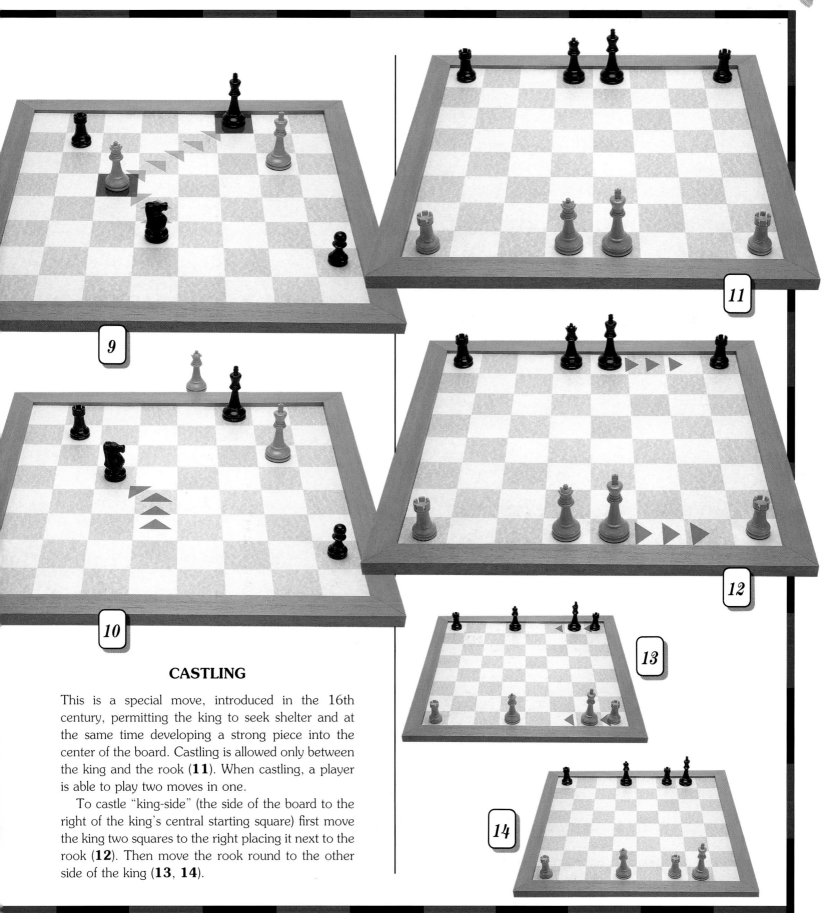

CASTLING

This is a special move, introduced in the 16th century, permitting the king to seek shelter and at the same time developing a strong piece into the center of the board. Castling is allowed only between the king and the rook (**11**). When castling, a player is able to play two moves in one.

To castle "king-side" (the side of the board to the right of the king's central starting square) first move the king two squares to the right placing it next to the rook (**12**). Then move the rook round to the other side of the king (**13**, **14**).

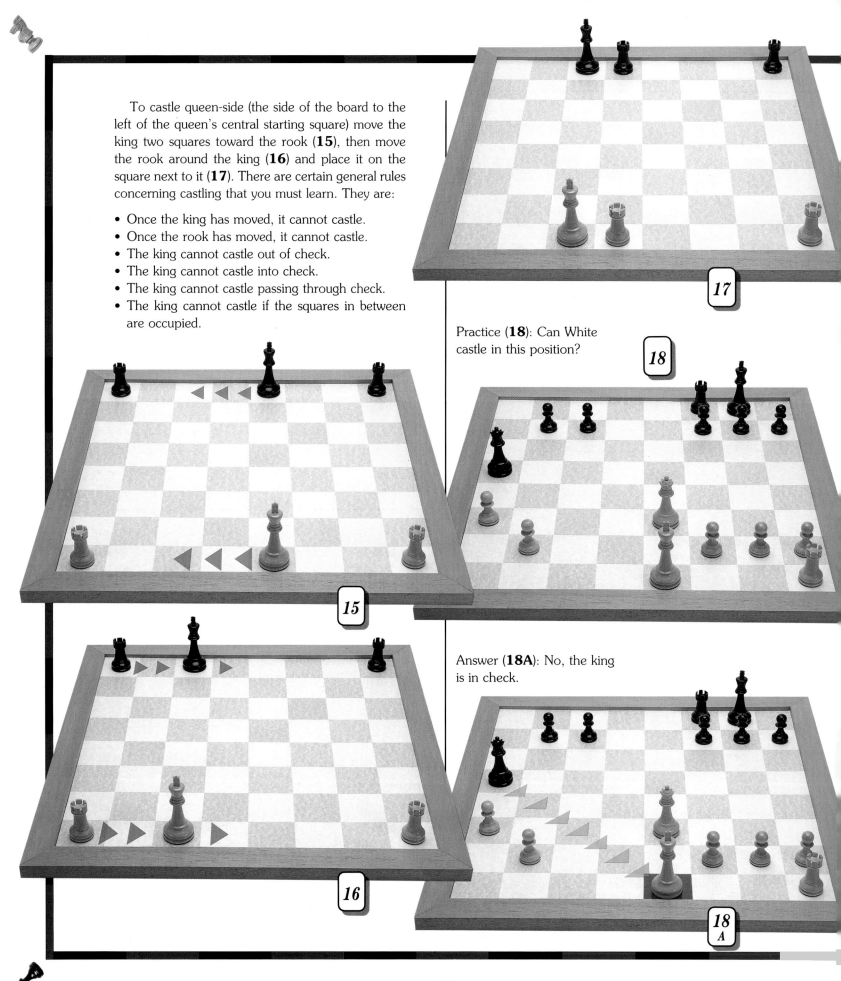

To castle queen-side (the side of the board to the left of the queen's central starting square) move the king two squares toward the rook (**15**), then move the rook around the king (**16**) and place it on the square next to it (**17**). There are certain general rules concerning castling that you must learn. They are:

- Once the king has moved, it cannot castle.
- Once the rook has moved, it cannot castle.
- The king cannot castle out of check.
- The king cannot castle into check.
- The king cannot castle passing through check.
- The king cannot castle if the squares in between are occupied.

Practice (**18**): Can White castle in this position?

Answer (**18A**): No, the king is in check.

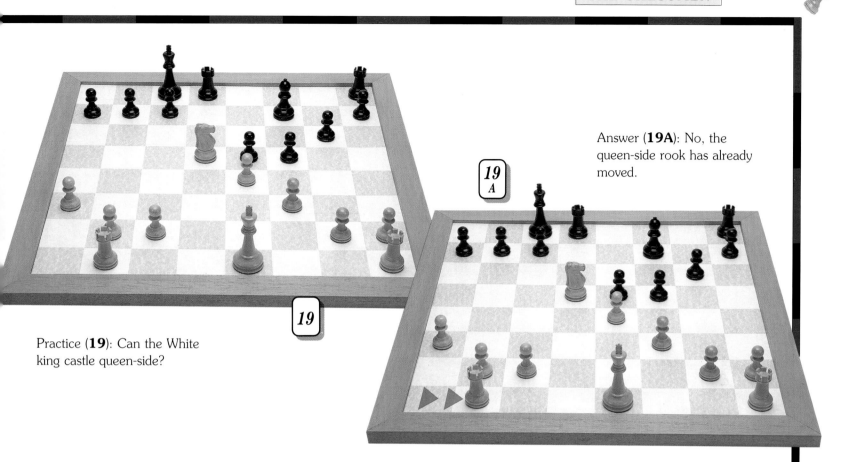

Answer (**19A**): No, the queen-side rook has already moved.

Practice (**19**): Can the White king castle queen-side?

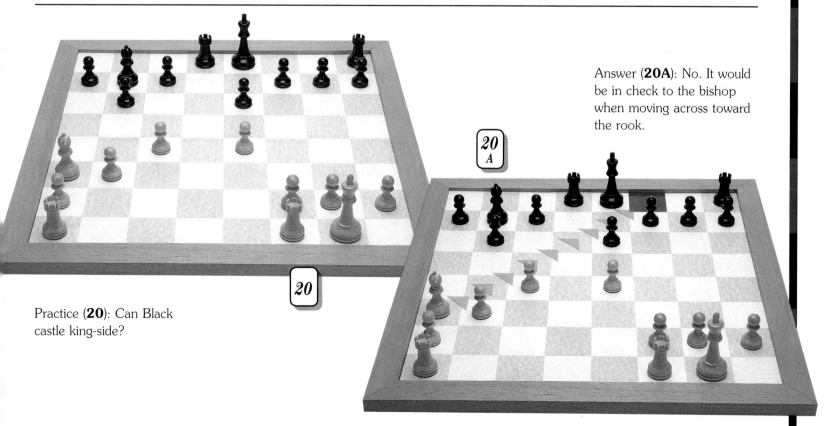

Answer (**20A**): No. It would be in check to the bishop when moving across toward the rook.

Practice (**20**): Can Black castle king-side?

OBTAINING A DRAWN GAME

There are a number circumstances in which a chess game will be drawn – that is, neither side will be able to achieve checkmate.

• *Insufficient material*. When there are insufficient chessmen left on the board for a checkmate. King v. king, king and knight v. king, king and bishop v. king are examples of this. But notice that king and pawn v. king are not among them as a pawn may be promoted if it reaches the eighth rank.

• *Perpetual check*. Occasionally a position is reached where every move can be check but checkmate cannot be forced. Then the game is drawn. Look at example (**21**). White wants to promote a pawn on the next move to win the game, but Black obtains a draw by forcing perpetual check with the queen. The White king is forced to move back and forth between the same two squares to get out of check (**22** - **25**), but Black can keep checking the king in the same way (**26**). It is perpetual check.

• *Repetition of position*. This is a very rare occurrence but the rules state that if the same position is repeated three times, not necessarily consecutively, it constitutes a draw. Perpetual check is also a repetition of position draw.

• *Fifty move rule*. This is a draw that can be claimed if no pawn has been moved and no capture made within fifty successive moves.

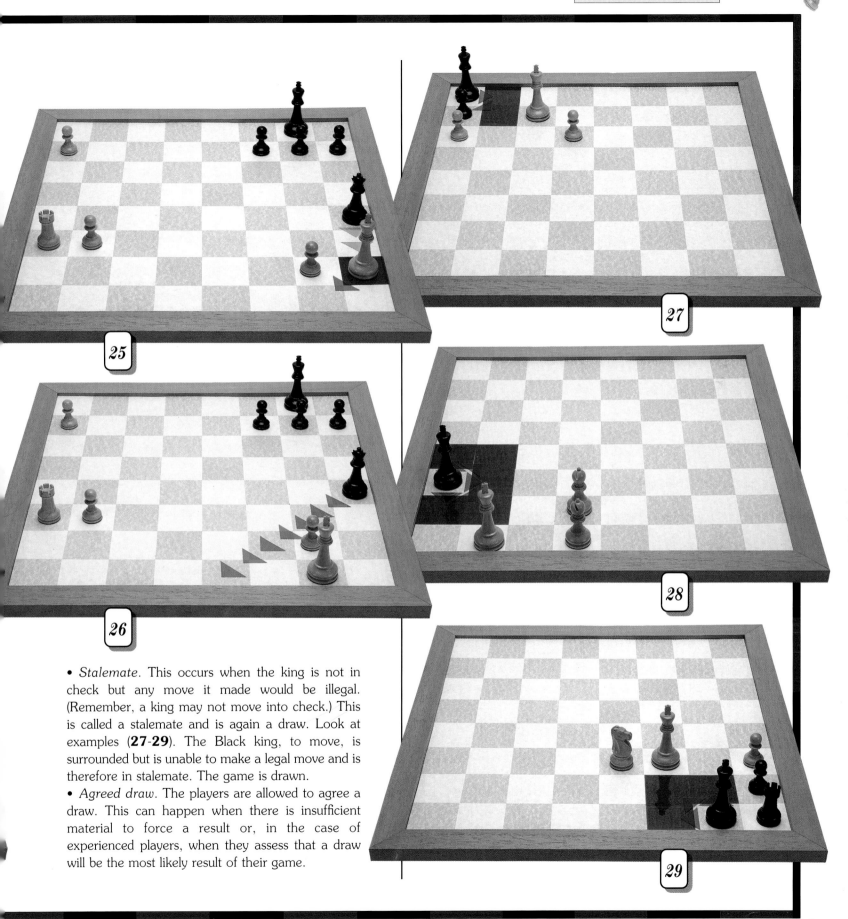

25

27

26

28

29

• *Stalemate*. This occurs when the king is not in check but any move it made would be illegal. (Remember, a king may not move into check.) This is called a stalemate and is again a draw. Look at examples (**27-29**). The Black king, to move, is surrounded but is unable to make a legal move and is therefore in stalemate. The game is drawn.

• *Agreed draw*. The players are allowed to agree a draw. This can happen when there is insufficient material to force a result or, in the case of experienced players, when they assess that a draw will be the most likely result of their game.

THE ENDGAME – CHECKMATE

Before explaining how the game is started and some basic rules of tactics, it is important that you know how to finish the game and gain a result. This is called the "endgame" and it is the subject of this chapter. When reading the previous section on the king, you will have learned that the king cannot be taken, unlike any other chess piece. Whenever the king is threatened, it has to be warned by calling – "check." This threat must be responded to immediately. On the next move the king must (if possible) get out of check. A king cannot give check. Kings always have to have at least a square separating them, and, of course, a king cannot move into check.

GETTING TO CHECKMATE

To win a game the king has to be checkmated. This is a feature not found in other board games and allows for exciting tactical complications, including imaginative sacrifices of other pieces undertaken in an attempt to checkmate the king.

To capture or checkmate the king, certain conditions have to apply:
- It has to be in check.
- It is unable to move away to an adjoining square.
- No chess piece can be interposed.
- The checking piece cannot be captured.

If this position is reached, it is checkmate – the king is captured; the game is won. Example boards (**1-3**) show a simple checkmate. The queen moves up to the Black king, checking it (**2**). It cannot be taken as the White king is protecting it. The Black king has no escape square, so it is checkmate (**3**).

FORCING CHECKMATE

The queen and rook are known as *major pieces* – they are the only individual chessmen, on an otherwise cleared board, that can force mate with solely the help of their king. When a game reaches the stage when only a few pieces remain, the pawns become very important. It is the side that can first promote a pawn to a queen (or rook) that will normally win. A king must have the assistance of at

Above: Political checkmate – Napoleon outwits Cornwallis over treaty negotiations in 1802.

least one of the major pieces to force checkmate.

Let us look at some examples of how to force checkmate against a lone king. First, how to do it when you have king and pawn v. king. In this circumstance, it is vital to promote the pawn to a queen. An endgame could result in a chase between the opposing king and pawn for the eighth rank. The Square is a simple method to calculate who will win the chase. Imagine a square on the board from the pawn's position to the eighth rank, and to where the opposing king stands (**4**). If the king can move into this square on the first move, it will catch the pawn and take it, but if not, the pawn queens. So, in this example, if it is White to move, White wins (**5**). Black to move, however, means the pawn can be captured (**6**) and Black can draw the game (lone kings only left on the board). White must try for this position (**7**) to

1

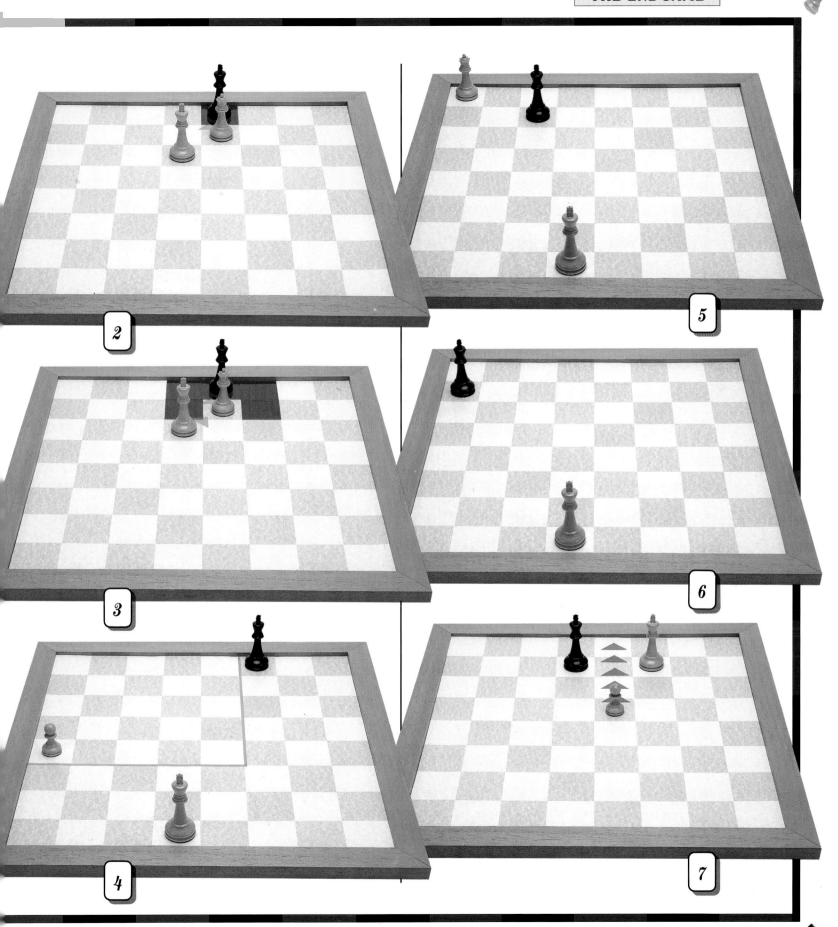

force the pawn through to queen. Black can often draw against the single pawn. For instance, in example (**8**) the Black king is stalemated in the corner, while in (**9**) the Black king controls the queening square.

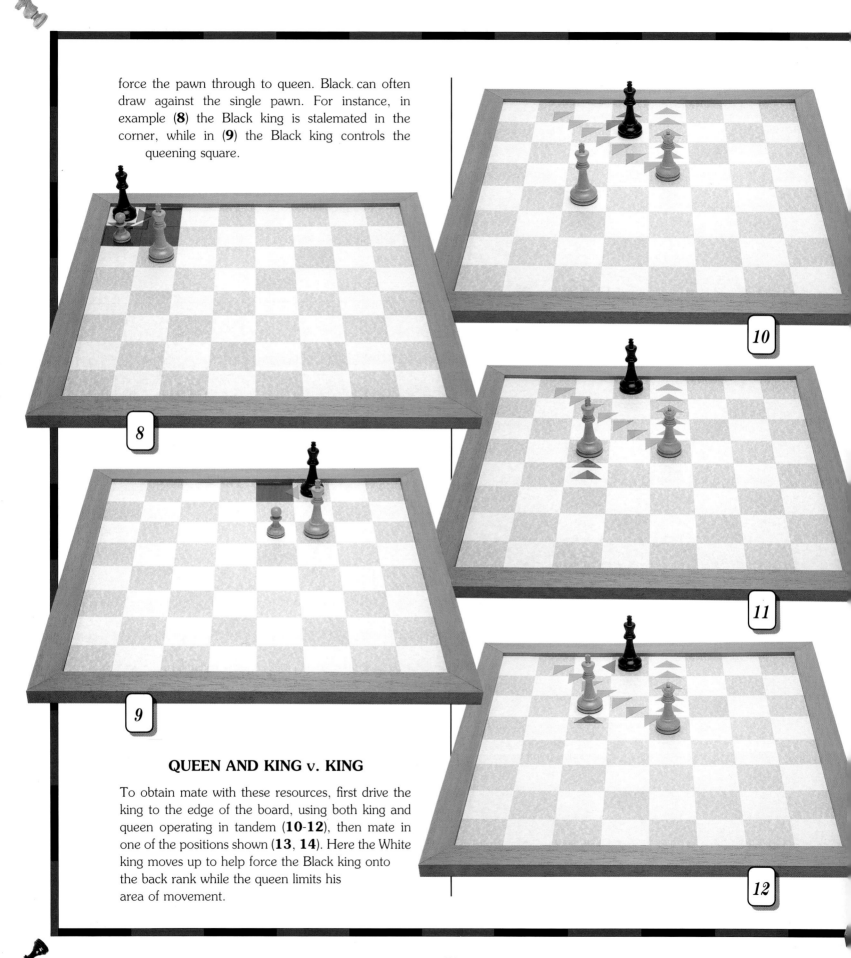

8

10

9

11

QUEEN AND KING v. KING

To obtain mate with these resources, first drive the king to the edge of the board, using both king and queen operating in tandem (**10-12**), then mate in one of the positions shown (**13**, **14**). Here the White king moves up to help force the Black king onto the back rank while the queen limits his area of movement.

12

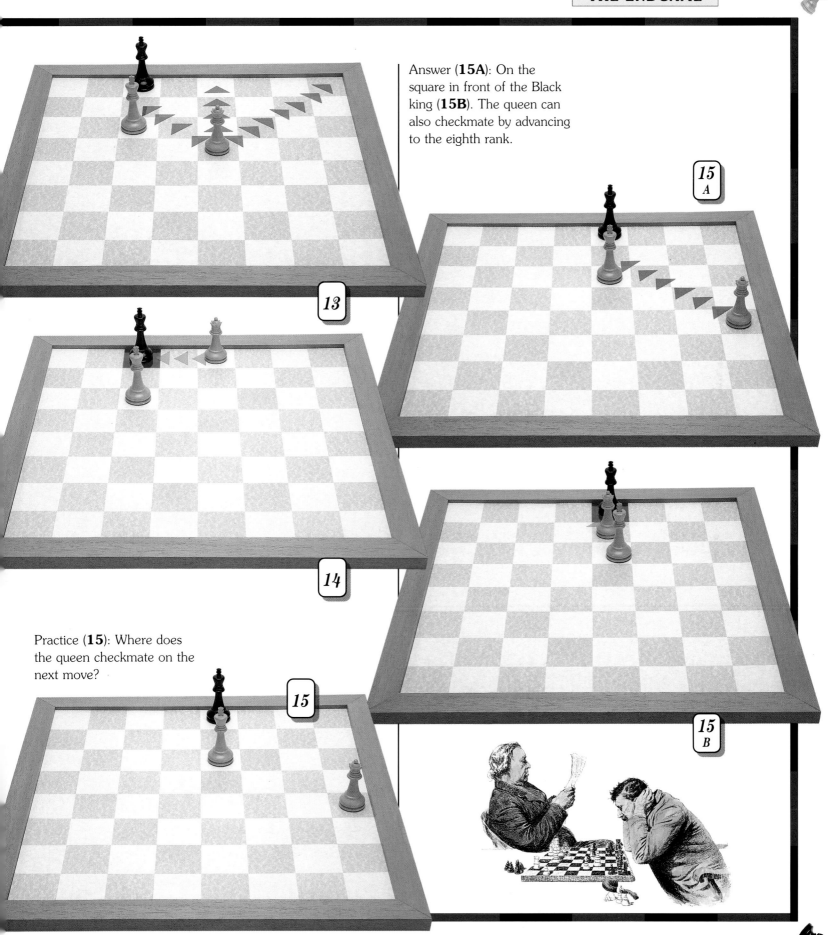

Answer (**15A**): On the square in front of the Black king (**15B**). The queen can also checkmate by advancing to the eighth rank.

Practice (**15**): Where does the queen checkmate on the next move?

Above: In this cartoon by R. Hogfeldt the unhappy Black king is checkmated by the White queen supported by her knight on the back rank.

ROOK AND KING v. KING

The general principle is the same for the rook as for the queen. With rook and king drive the lone king to the side of the board or into a corner, then mate using a waiting move to force the king on to the mating square. In the example (**16-22**), the king is forced onto the eighth file by the rook without a check (**16-19**). The White king then moves into position (**20**) and then the rook moves (**21**) to give checkmate (**22**).

16

17

18

19

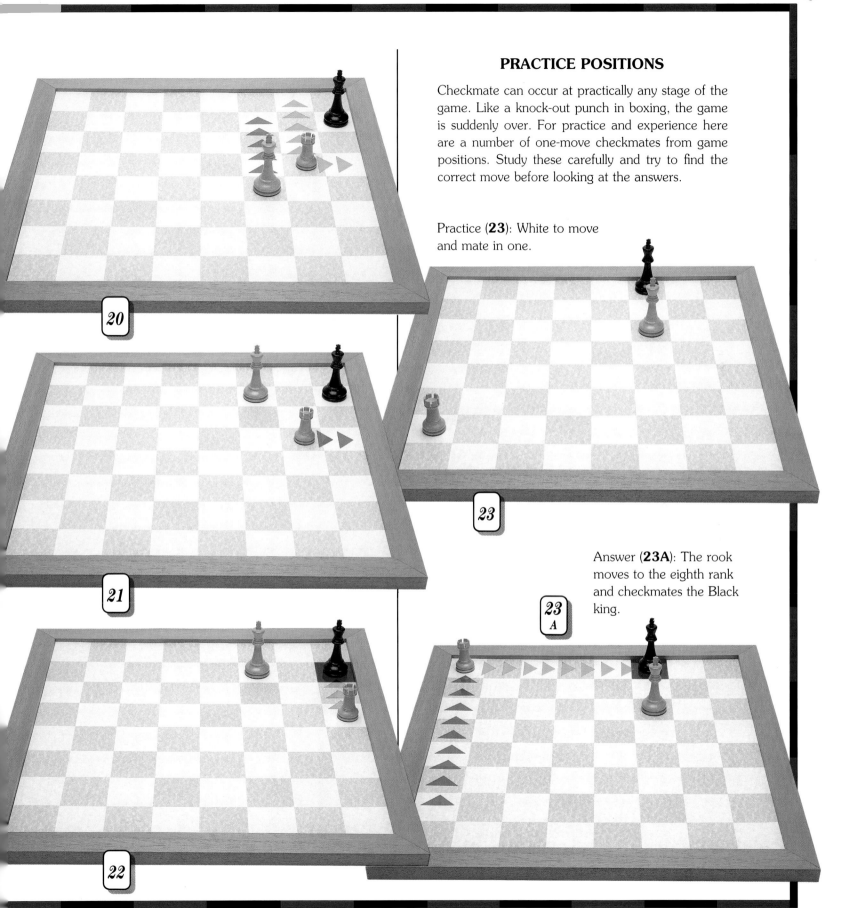

PRACTICE POSITIONS

Checkmate can occur at practically any stage of the game. Like a knock-out punch in boxing, the game is suddenly over. For practice and experience here are a number of one-move checkmates from game positions. Study these carefully and try to find the correct move before looking at the answers.

Practice (**23**): White to move and mate in one.

Answer (**23A**): The rook moves to the eighth rank and checkmates the Black king.

59

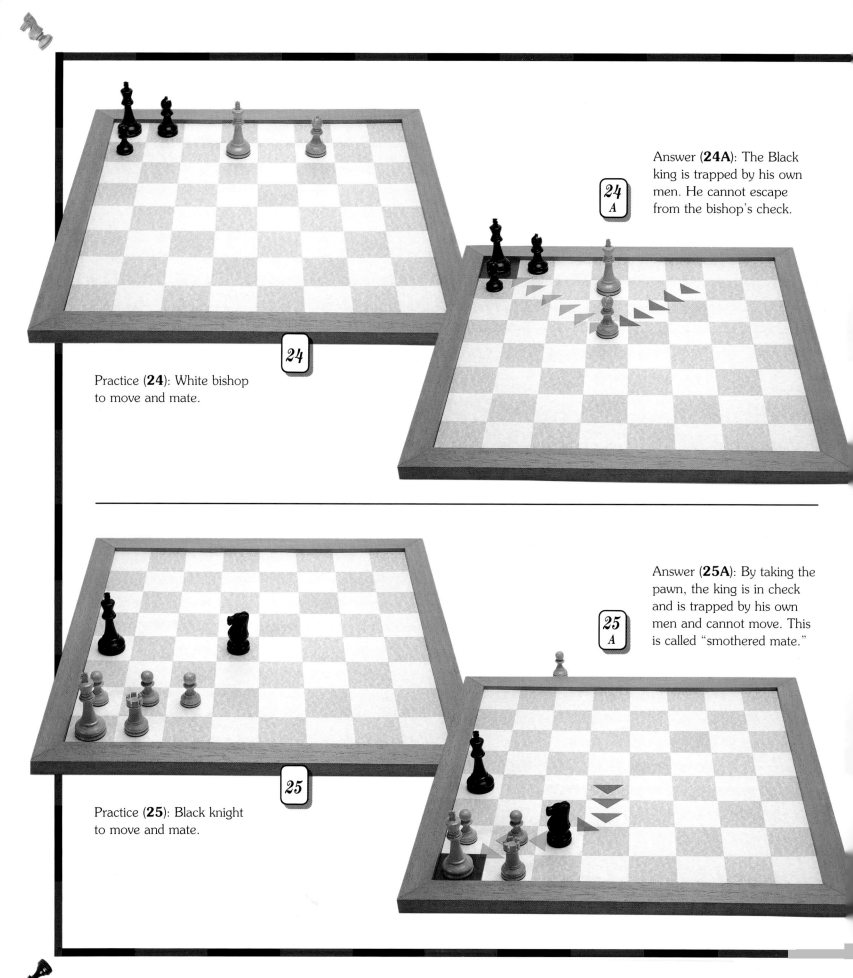

Answer (**24A**): The Black king is trapped by his own men. He cannot escape from the bishop's check.

Practice (**24**): White bishop to move and mate.

Answer (**25A**): By taking the pawn, the king is in check and is trapped by his own men and cannot move. This is called "smothered mate."

Practice (**25**): Black knight to move and mate.

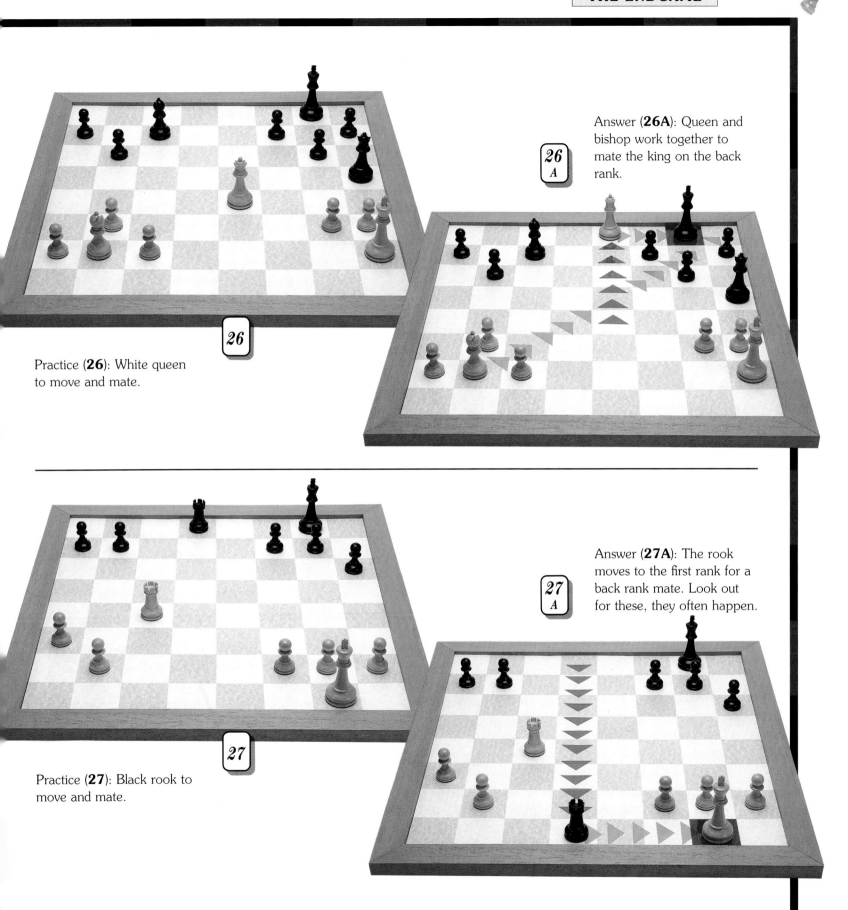

Answer (**26A**): Queen and bishop work together to mate the king on the back rank.

Practice (**26**): White queen to move and mate.

Answer (**27A**): The rook moves to the first rank for a back rank mate. Look out for these, they often happen.

Practice (**27**): Black rook to move and mate.

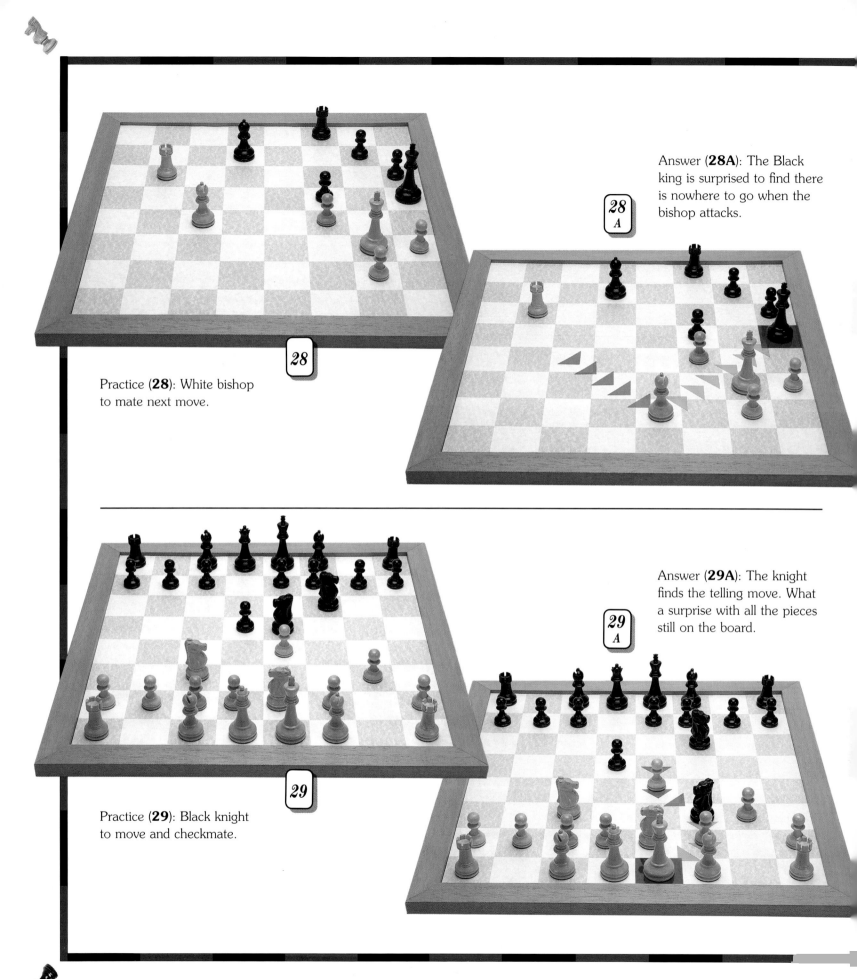

Answer (**28A**): The Black king is surprised to find there is nowhere to go when the bishop attacks.

Practice (**28**): White bishop to mate next move.

Answer (**29A**): The knight finds the telling move. What a surprise with all the pieces still on the board.

Practice (**29**): Black knight to move and checkmate.

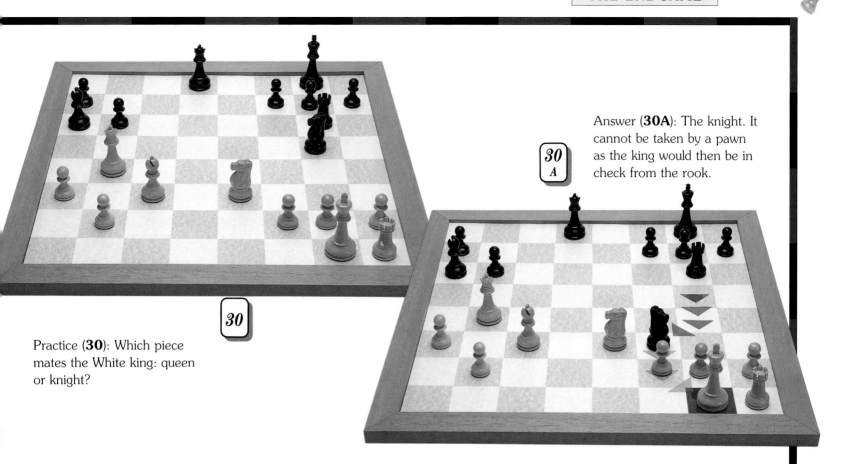

Answer (**30A**): The knight. It cannot be taken by a pawn as the king would then be in check from the rook.

Practice (**30**): Which piece mates the White king: queen or knight?

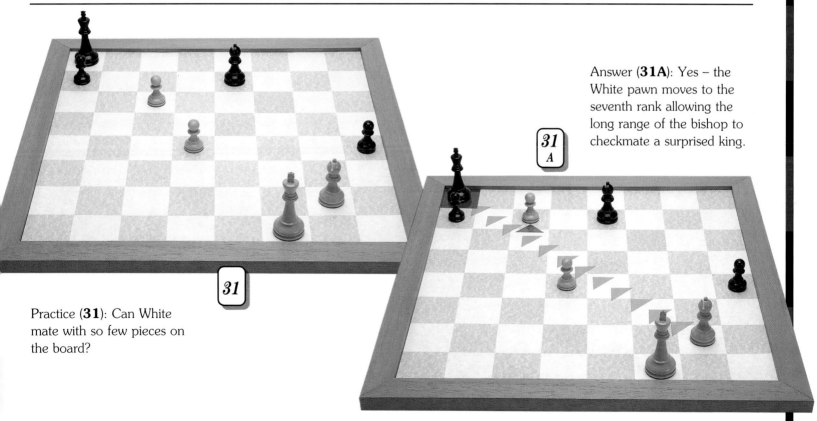

Answer (**31A**): Yes – the White pawn moves to the seventh rank allowing the long range of the bishop to checkmate a surprised king.

Practice (**31**): Can White mate with so few pieces on the board?

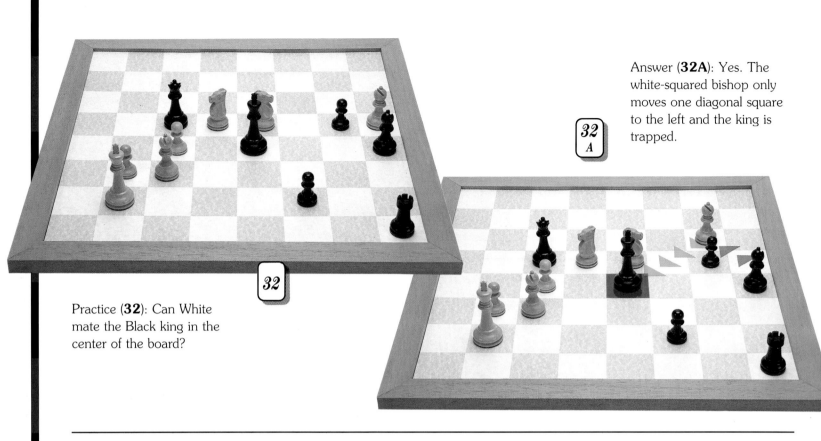

Answer (**32A**): Yes. The white-squared bishop only moves one diagonal square to the left and the king is trapped.

Practice (**32**): Can White mate the Black king in the center of the board?

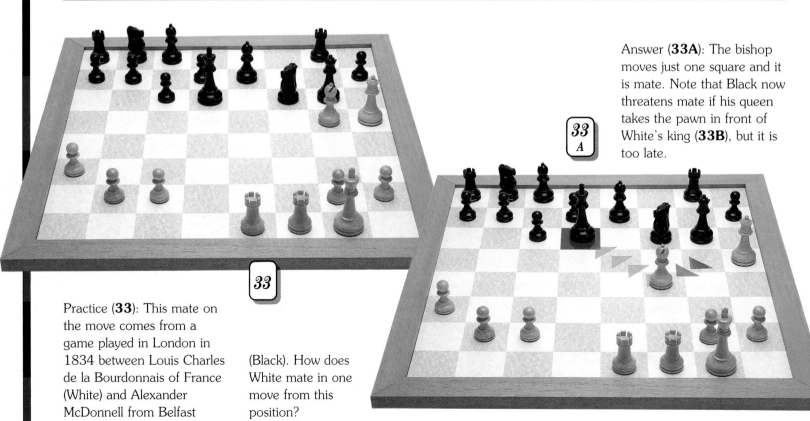

Answer (**33A**): The bishop moves just one square and it is mate. Note that Black now threatens mate if his queen takes the pawn in front of White's king (**33B**), but it is too late.

Practice (**33**): This mate on the move comes from a game played in London in 1834 between Louis Charles de la Bourdonnais of France (White) and Alexander McDonnell from Belfast (Black). How does White mate in one move from this position?

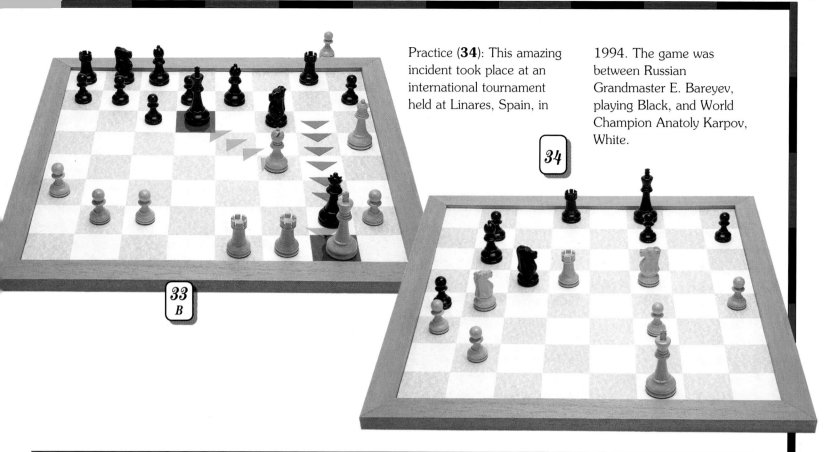

Practice (**34**): This amazing incident took place at an international tournament held at Linares, Spain, in 1994. The game was between Russian Grandmaster E. Bareyev, playing Black, and World Champion Anatoly Karpov, White.

Answer (**35A**): The White rook takes the Black rook – mate. This is a true lesson; no matter how expert one is at chess, there is no immunity from human error!

In an even position Bareyev played the move illustrated (**35**) and Karpov had little difficulty in finding a mate in one. What move was it?

READING MODERN CHESS NOTATION

Chess is fortunate that for over a thousand years games and problems have been preserved, because methods of recording the moves were established and have been passed down to us. The earliest kind of chess notation was introduced by the Arabs during the 9th and 10th centuries. It is called the Algebraic system. When chess came to Europe, a different form of recording moves – Descriptive Notation – was used until the 18th century, when the Algebraic form was reintroduced by the Syrian Phillip Stamma of Aleppo and adopted in the German-speaking countries. Since then both systems have been popular and have proved to be excellent for recording chess games. This chapter explains them both.

ALGEBRAIC NOTATION

In 1976 the World Chess Federation decided to recognize only one official system of notation for its tournaments and matches. They chose the Algebraic system, and this is now the method in general use. Once the Algebraic method is understood, games and problems can be followed in the national press and in chess magazines. Even games in foreign languages become readily understandable. In particular, learning this system will help beginners to study and understand the games of gifted chess players.

The pieces are identified by using their initial letter, except for the knight which, having the same initial letter as the king, is either known as N or occasionally Kt. So we find K for king, Q for Queen, B for bishop, N for knight, R for rook and P for pawn (**1**).

| R | B | Q | K | N | P |

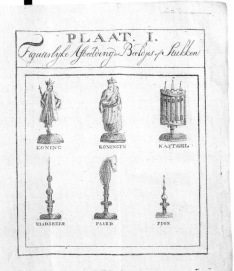

Left: This illustration of chessmen is from a Dutch translation of Philidor's classic text of 1749 *L'Analyze du Jeu des Échecs* which was published in this edition in Holland in 1819.

Each square on the board is identified by two co-ordinates. The letters a to h run along the lower horizontal edge of the board identifying each file (**2**). The numbers 1 to 8 are similarly shown on the left-hand vertical edge of the board identifying each rank (**3**). So White's queen-side rook occupies square a1 at the start of a game. Often boards and diagrams show these markings as an aid to recording the moves. Diagrams will always show White playing from the first rank and Black from the top rank (**4**).

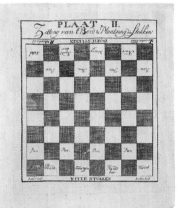

Left: This is Plate II from the Dutch edition of Philidor. It shows how the chessmen should be placed at the start of a game. The form of notation is descriptive; the pieces' names are overprinted on the appropriate squares.

	a	b	c	d	e	f	g	h	
8	a8	b8	c8	d8	e8	f8	g8	h8	8
7	a7	b7	c7	d7	e7	f7	g7	h7	7
6	a6	b6	c6	d6	e6	f6	g6	h6	6
5	a5	b5	c5	d5	e5	f5	g5	h5	5
4	a4	b4	c4	d4	e4	f4	g4	h4	4
3	a3	b3	c3	d3	e3	f3	g3	h3	3
2	a2	b2	c2	d2	e2	f2	g2	h2	2
1	a1	b1	c1	d1	e1	f1	g1	h1	1
	a	b	c	d	e	f	g	h	

Above: A board with algebraic notation added to it. Each square has its own "grid reference" for recording chess moves.

In summaries of games, pairs of moves are numbered from 1 onward, White's moves being given first. The description starts with the initial letter of the piece being moved and then gives the co-ordinates of the square to which it has moved. When two similar pieces could move to the same destination square, then part of the co-ordinate of the departure square is also given. So, Ra7 means that the rook moves to square a7, while Nbd7 means the knight on the b file moves to square d7. In the case of pawns, the initial letter "P" is often left out, the destination square being sufficient to identify the move. So, e4 means that the pawn on the e file has moved to square e4.

Certain other symbols are included in the notation system to indicate other events in the game. They are listed below:

x	capture
+	check
=	pawn promotion
o-o	king-side castling
o-o-o	queen-side castling
?	bad move
!	good move
...	Black's move
e.p.	en passant

SCHOLAR'S MATE

This is an opening to be played for fun and to give you a chance of practicing reading notation. It only lasts four moves, assuming your opponent is careless. It was named "Scholar's Mate" in 1614 with the advice "it is a scholar's mate, but there is no man of judgement in chess-play will take such a mate."

1. e4   e5 (**5**)
2. Bc4   Bc5 (**6**)
3. Qf3   Nc6 (**7**)
4. Qxf7+ mate (**8**)

Right: The world's leading players of the 1880s. Blackburne is sitting in the left-hand corner next to Steinitz who faces Zukertort over the board.

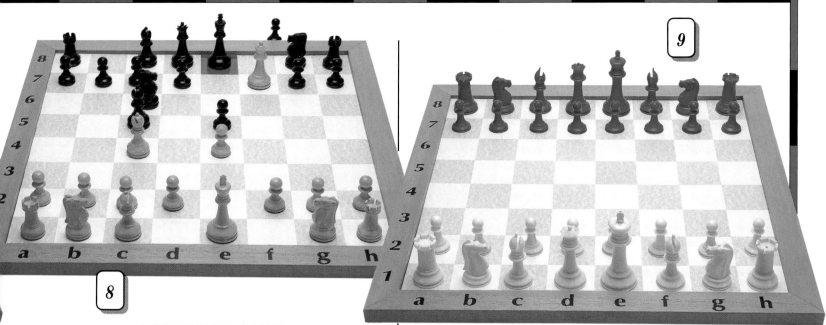

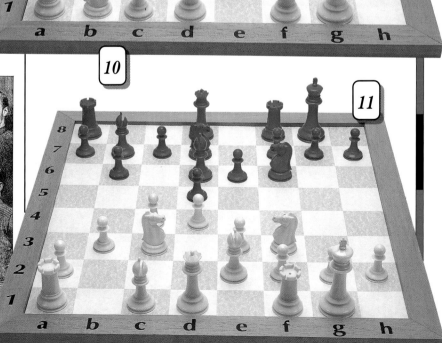

A BRILLIANT GAME

To continue practicing notation, follow this exciting game between Johannes Zukertort, the outstanding winner of the 1883 London International Tournament and Joseph Blackburne, nicknamed the "Black Death" by the German masters, due to his brilliant and sudden knock-out combinations.

The red and white ivory chess set illustrating this game (**9**) is the actual one that they used in 1883. It became the property of Zukertort at an auction held at the end of the tournament.

Zukertort (White), Blackburne (Black), English Opening.

1.	c4	e6	2. e3	Nf6
3.	Nf3	b6	4. Be2	Bb7
5.	o-o	d5 (**10**)	6. d4	Bd6
7.	Nc3	o-o	8. b3	Nbd7 (**11**)

Here the knight's starting square is indicated as both knights could move to d7.

      9. Bb2 Qe7   10. Nb5 Ne4 (**12**)

In the opening both players have been bringing their pieces into play concentrating on controlling the center, and castling so that their kings are in a strong defensive position.

      11. Nxd6 cxd6 (**13**)

The first captures. White has an advantage as two bishops are considered to be slightly better than two knights. It is not always necessary to indicate the pieces involved in the capture. Black's move can be recorded as simply as cd.

      12. Nd2 Ndf6

Again both knights could move to f6 so the piece's starting square is indicated to avoid confusion.

13. f3	Nxd2	14. Qxd2	dxc (**14**)
15. Bxc4	d5	16. Bd3	Rfc8
17. Rae1	Rc7	18. e4	Rac8 (**15**)

White is developing an attack through the center while Black is preparing to counterattack on the c file.

19. e5	Ne8	20. f4	g6
21. Re3	f5	22. exf e.p.	Nxf6 (**16**)
			(en passant)
23. f5	Ne4	24. Bxe4	dxe4
25. fxg	Rc2 (**17**)		

Rook threatens both queen and bishop.

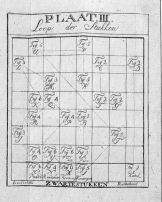

Right: Plate III from the Dutch edition of Philidor shows the legal move of each chessman. This form of notation is pictorial rather than descriptive.

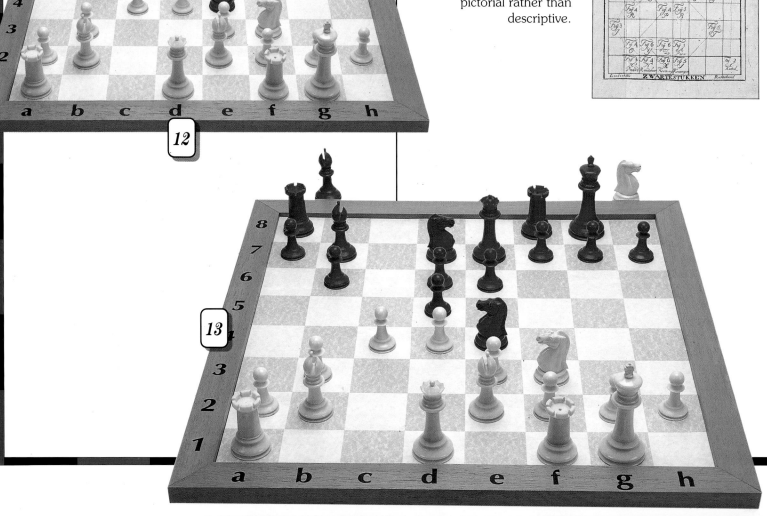

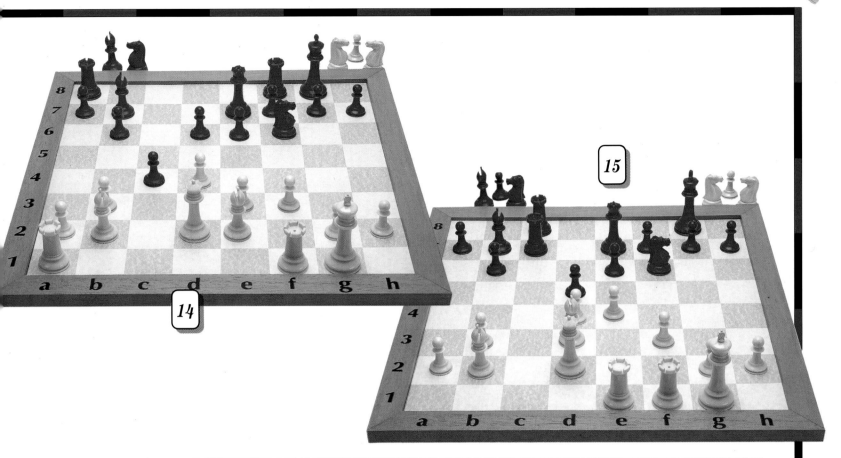

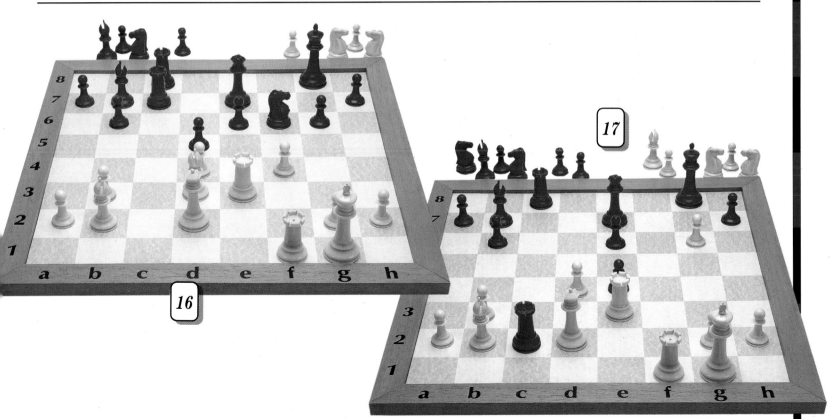

26. gxh+(check)   Kh8

(If . . .Kxh7 27. Rh3 gives check from rook followed by an overwhelming attack.)

27. d5+   e5   28. Qb4!! (**18**)

This is a brilliant offer of a queen sacrifice which cannot be accepted. As Blackburne wrote at the time "If the queen is taken, White has a mate in seven moves."

28. . . . R8c5 (**19**)

He thought this strong reply would win the game for Black – another victim of the "Black Death." However,

29. Rf8+!!   Kxh7 (**20**)

Another sacrifice that cannot be taken. (After 29. . . Qxf8 30. Bxe5+ Kxh7 31. Qxe4+ Kh6 32. Rh3 with mate to follow.)

30. Qxe4+   Kg7

31. Bxe5+   Kxf8 (**21**)

32. Bg7+ Resigns (**22**)

In tournament games a player will "Resign" when he believes his game is completely lost, making it unnecessary to play on until he is mated. In this game Blackburne saw . . .Qxg7 33. Qe8 checkmate (**23**).

DESCRIPTIVE NOTATION

Descriptive notation is still being used by some chess columnists, and most of the earlier chess books in English use this system. Therefore, for further study, it will be helpful to know this alternative method of notation.

The names of the pieces are abbreviated as follows:

K = King. Q = Queen. R = Rook. Kt or N = Knight. B = Bishop. P = Pawn.

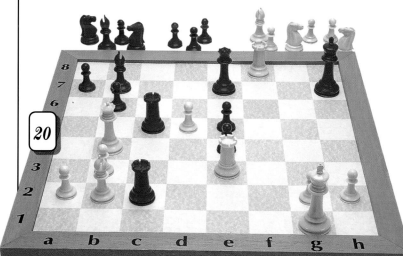

22

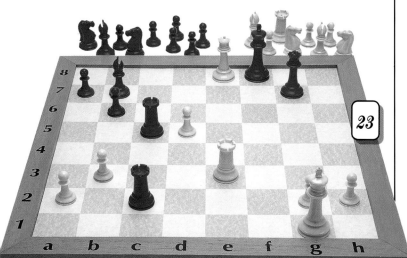

23

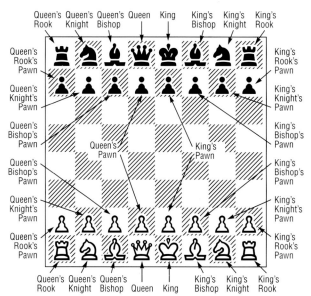

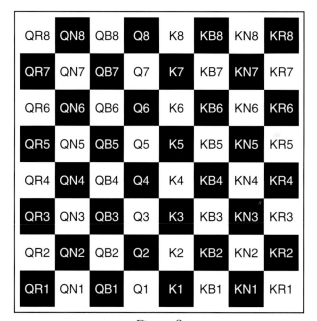

Figure 1

Figure 2

THE NAMES OF THE SQUARES

Each square has two names, one used by White and one by Black. Look at the board from White's starting position. Each square is named by the piece that stands on it. Starting from the right-hand corner, the first square is the King's Rook square, abbreviated to KR1, the next square is KN1, followed by KB1 and K1. This continues on the Queen's side of the board as Q1, QB1, QN1, QR1 (see Figure 1). Each piece also identifies each square along the file. On the King's file for example, the squares are numbered K1, K2, K3 continuing until the eighth square K8 (see Figure 2). For Black, the names are the same but are recorded from Black's starting position.

Each pawn uses the name of the file it occupies. Starting a game with the king's pawn, White would write down P-K4 and Black could reply with P-KB4. Note that he would not write P-B4 as this could mean either the QB file or the KB file. When a pawn captures a piece and so changes its file, its name alters correspondingly.

When capturing, the sign x is used, e.g. QxN or PxP etc., o-o and o-o-o mean castling king-side and queen-side respectively, + is check, ++ checkmate.

TACTICS

A tactic is an element in your overall plan of a game of chess by which you try to gain advantage over your opponent. It can be as simple as making a move which threatens an opponent's unprotected piece. However, not too many games are going to be won relying heavily on this play. The game mainly consists of perceptible tactics working in harmony, which on occasion will create positions of pure intellectual beauty. Put simply, most games are won through tactics. There are a few general motifs that occur regularly and with practice they will become familiar to you. During a game there will be opportunities to set tactical traps. The most effective of these are the Fork, the Pin and the Skewer, together with Discovered Attacks, Overloading, and Sacrifices. This chapter explains what they are and how to apply them effectively during play.

THE FORK

This is a tactic that is available to each piece. Two or more chessmen on the opposing side are attacked simultaneously by one piece. In example (**1**) a rook and queen are "forked" simultaneously by a knight. One will be taken.

The queen is a particularly useful piece when it comes to forking. Being the most powerful chess piece it can, when in a central position, fork simultaneously in many directions. In example (**2**) the White queen forks both rook and bishop. The Black queen forks a knight with check on the king (**3**).

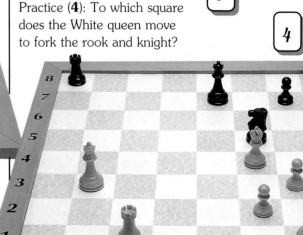

Practice (**4**): To which square does the White queen move to fork the rook and knight?

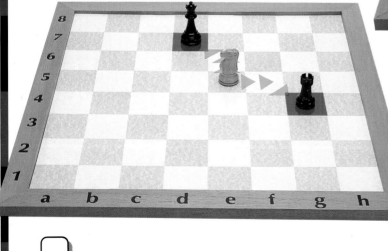

Answer (**4A**): d5.

Practice (**7**): The White bishop finds a decisive fork, on which square?

Since the bishop moves diagonally on its own color squares, it is ideal for forking. In example (**5**) for instance, the White bishop forks two rooks. In (**6**) the Black bishop forks a knight and rook.

Answer (**7A**): f4.

The fork is the only tactic a knight can employ. Placed in the center of a board, it forks onto eight different squares. Combine this with the power to jump at an angle, and the knight fork is well disguised. In example (**8**) the White knight at the edge of the board forks the queen, pawn and rook simultaneously. In (**9**) the Black knight forks four pieces – queen, rook, bishop and pawn.

Answer (**10A**): d5.

Working along the files and ranks, the rook often traps two pieces in a fork. In example (**11**) the White rook traps a pawn and bishop in a right-angle threat. In (**12**) the Black rook traps a bishop and knight on a file.

Practice (**10**): The White knight moves onto a central square and forks three pieces. Which square?

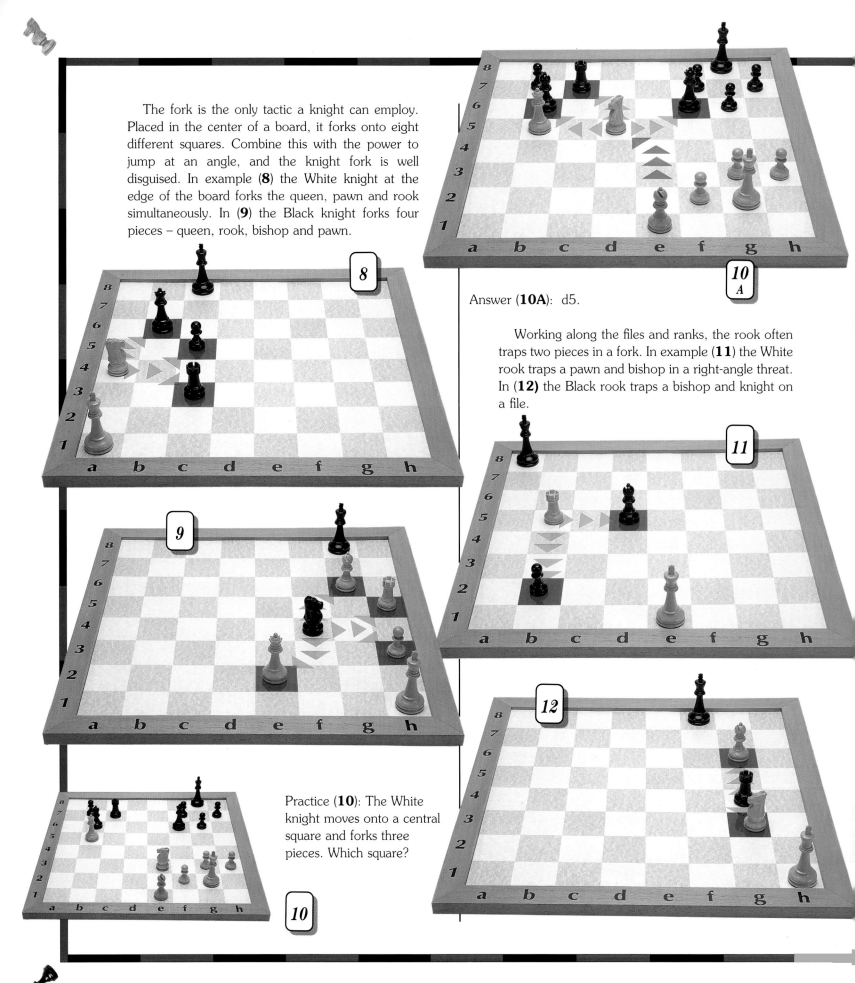

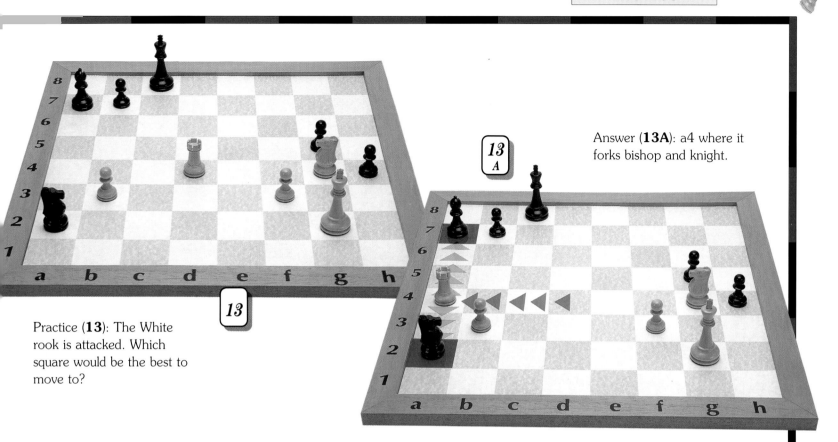

Answer (**13A**): a4 where it forks bishop and knight.

Practice (**13**): The White rook is attacked. Which square would be the best to move to?

The way in which a pawn takes pieces diagonally allows it to fork simultaneously in two directions. For example, here (**14**) a White pawn forks queen and knight. In (**15**) a Black pawn forks both White knights.

THE SKEWER

This is an attack upon two pieces on the same line. One is "skewered" behind a valuable piece on its own side and will be taken when that piece has to move. Look at example (**16**). The Black king must move as it is in check from White's bishop, allowing for the capture of the queen behind.

THE PIN

This works on the same principle as the skewer, but here it is the first piece on a line that is captured, pinned against a more valuable chessman behind that must not be exposed. In example (**18**) the White queen has pinned the bishop against its king. In (**19**) the White knight is pinned by the Black queen against a rook, so it can be taken by Black's pawn.

16

17 A

Answer (**17A**): b4.

17

Practice (**17**): To which square should the White bishop move to skewer a knight through a rook?

78

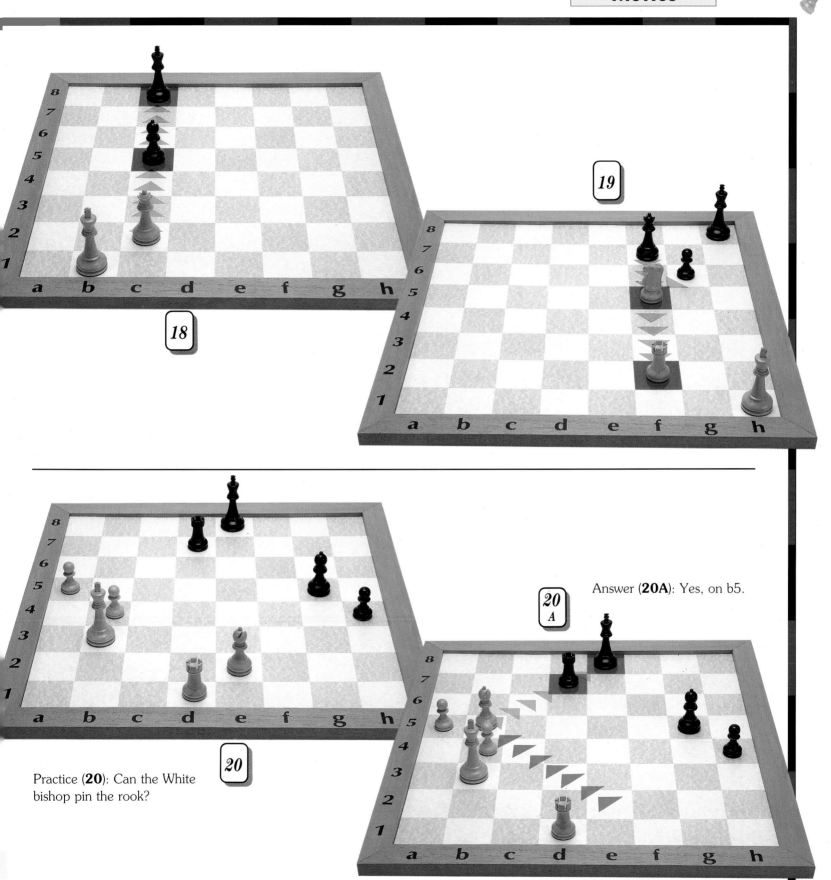

18

19

20

20
A

Answer (**20A**): Yes, on b5.

Practice (**20**): Can the White bishop pin the rook?

DISCOVERED ATTACK

This is an ambush, particularly strong if a "check" is also involved. It happens when a piece is moved to reveal an attack by another piece on the same side against an opposing piece. For example, look at board (**21**). The White rook and bishop are on the same file as the Black king. The bishop can move to attack another piece and Black has to reply to the discovered check from the rook (**22**). In example (**23**) the Black knight and bishop are on the same diagonal as the White king. If the knight moves to attack the White rook, the king is in check from the bishop (**24**).

Practice (**25**): The White bishop and rook are on the same diagonal as the Black king. How can White, to move, take advantage of this?

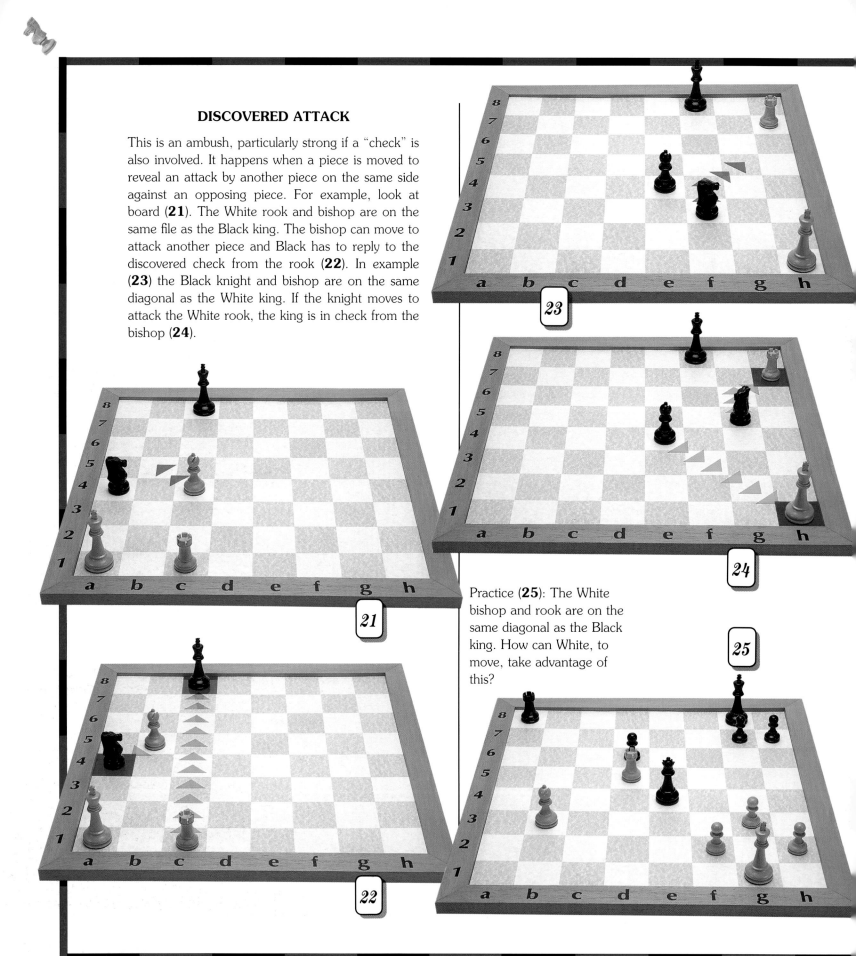

80

Answer (**25A**): Rook to d4
or e5 wins the queen.

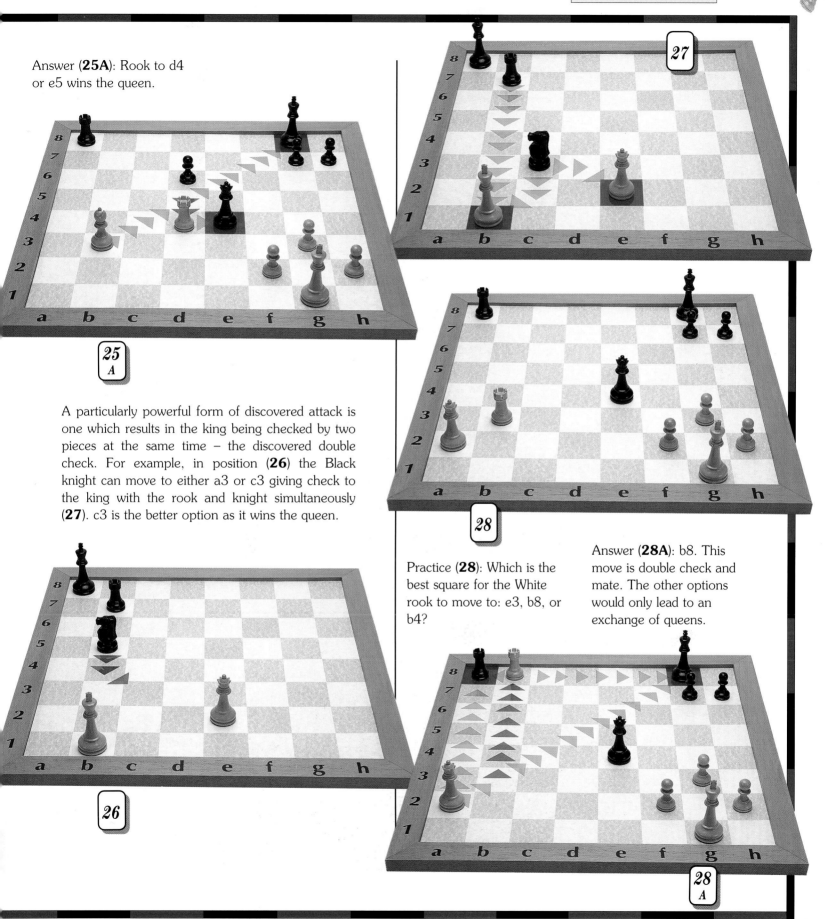

A particularly powerful form of discovered attack is one which results in the king being checked by two pieces at the same time – the discovered double check. For example, in position (**26**) the Black knight can move to either a3 or c3 giving check to the king with the rook and knight simultaneously (**27**). c3 is the better option as it wins the queen.

Practice (**28**): Which is the best square for the White rook to move to: e3, b8, or b4?

Answer (**28A**): b8. This move is double check and mate. The other options would only lead to an exchange of queens.

81

OVERLOADING

One piece may have to defend more than one other piece on its own side. An attack on these chessmen can cause "overloading." If one piece is taken, the recapturing of the attacker's piece will leave another undefended – a victim of the overload. Look at example (**29**). The Black knight is defending a rook and bishop which are under attack from the White queen and rook respectively. When the Black bishop is taken by the rook, which is recaptured by the knight (**30**), the Black rook is left undefended from being taken by the White queen (**31**).

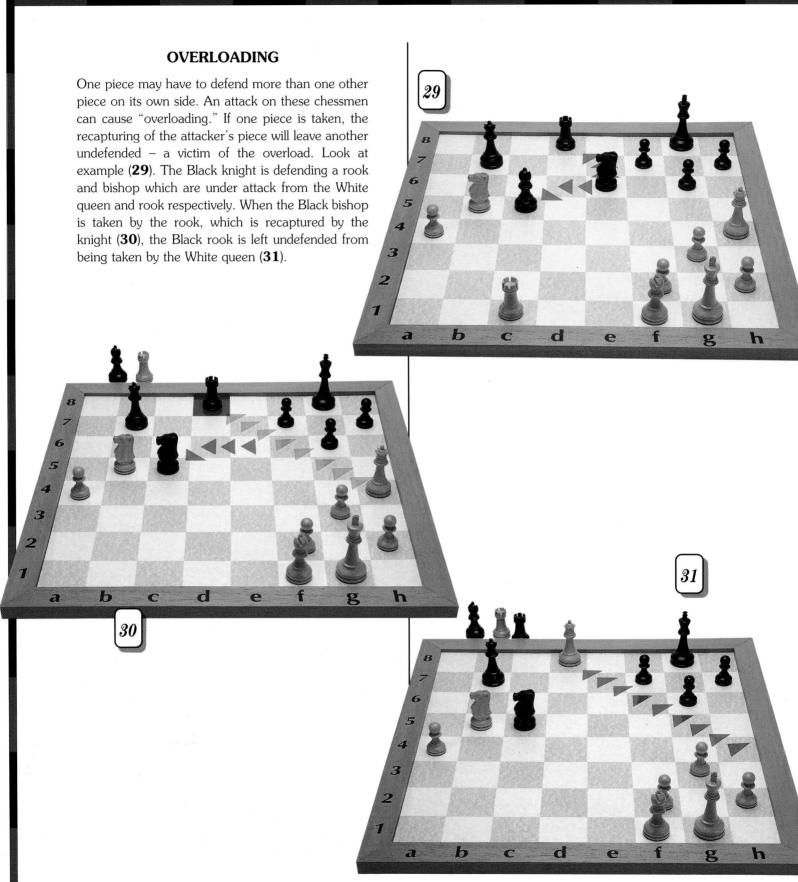

Answer (**32A**): Bishop should take knight. Then QxB (**32B**) and NxB (**32C**). (If NxB, NxN).

Practice (**32**): Even a queen can be overloaded. Which would be best for Black, to take the bishop with the knight or to take the knight with the bishop?

SACRIFICE

This is the ultimate tactic in chess – to calculate the deliberate giving up of a piece, or even a number of men, for positional or tactical advantage. Often this can lead to a direct attack on the king ending in checkmate or an overwhelming advantage. However, if the calculation is unsound, the reverse can happen and the game could be lost. Look at example board (**33**). The Black queen is sacrificed for the pawn on h2. The king has to take the queen (**34**). The knight moves to g3 with a discovered attack on the king from the rook. It must move to g1 (**35**). The rook moves to h1. Checkmate (**36**).

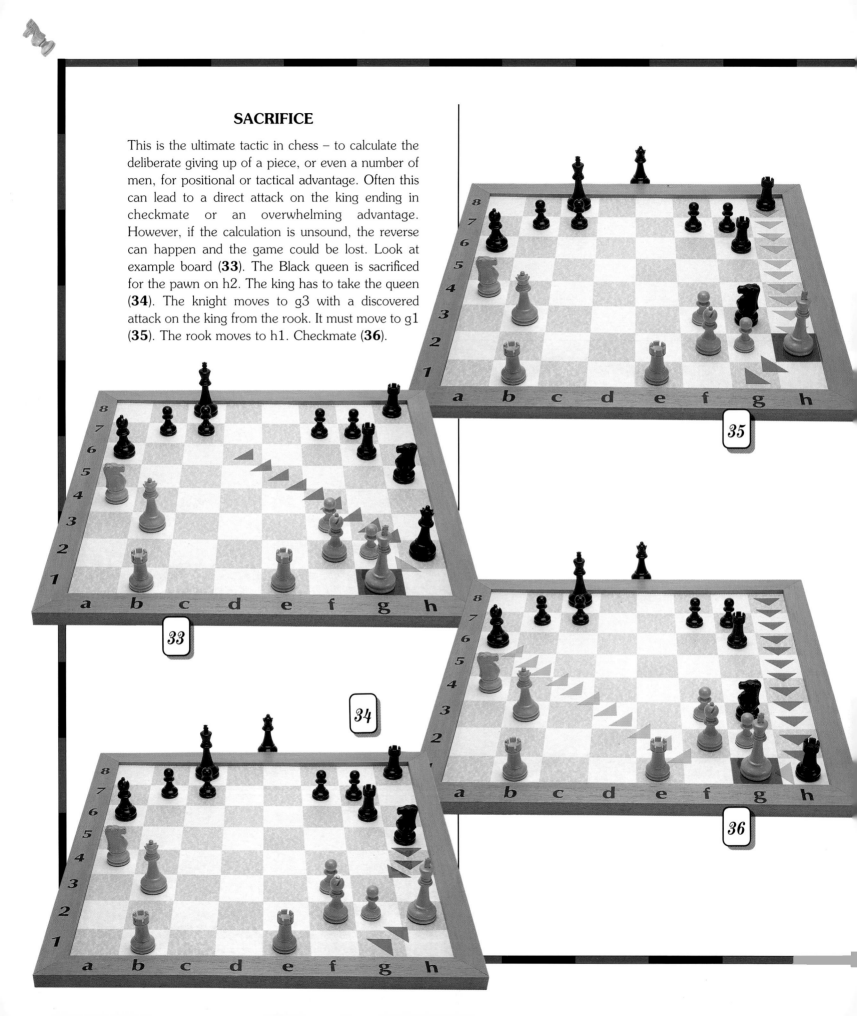

Answer (**37A**): Qg6+ Kf8 (**37B**). QxR mate (**37C**).

Practice (**37**): The White bishop sacrifices on f7. How does White now mate in two moves?

37

37 A

37 B

37 C

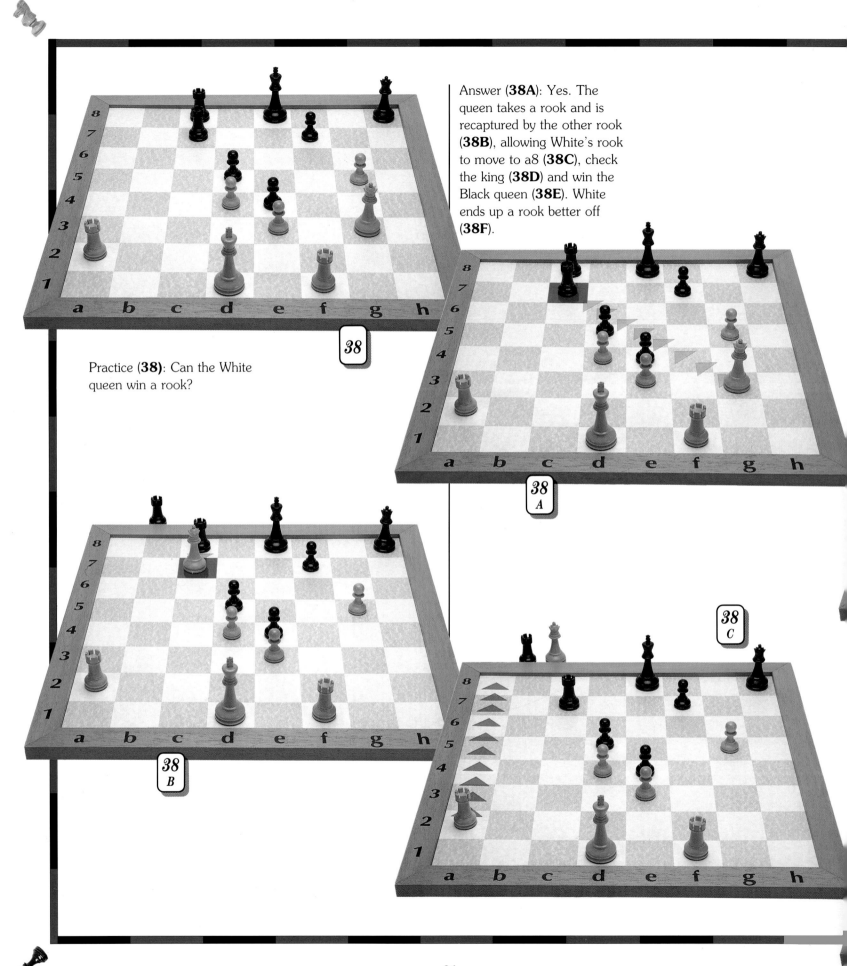

Practice (**38**): Can the White queen win a rook?

Answer (**38A**): Yes. The queen takes a rook and is recaptured by the other rook (**38B**), allowing White's rook to move to a8 (**38C**), check the king (**38D**) and win the Black queen (**38E**). White ends up a rook better off (**38F**).

GENERAL ADVICE

Obtain as much direct experience as possible by constantly playing with a partner. Use the book for reference. As problems arise, check the book for advice and use it for continual practice. Repetition is important in the assimilation of new experiences. Use two boards when studying, one to follow the main line and one to analyze the position.

Develop a pattern of concentration. Before each move check the position on the board to avoid silly errors, such as moving a piece to a square where it will be "en prise," a chess expression that means a piece is put in a position where it can be taken for no compensation.

Remember to castle early in the game, normally before the 10th move. Avoid "holes" in your position. A "hole" is a square in your half of the board that is unprotected, allowing an opposing piece to occupy it.

- Look for holes in your opponent's position
- Rooks work best on open files, and working together in combination.
- If you have gained the initiative, won a pawn or another piece, aim to exchange pieces. This will increase the advantage.
- Pawns work best in protective chains.
- Isolated pawns on their own are easy prey.
- Double pawns on a file can also be a weakness.
- Kings can be used like a strong piece in the endgame.

It is not to be expected that early on, without completely understanding the moves of the pieces, that all this advice can be assimilated or even properly understood. First some experience must be gained so you become thoroughly familiar with the individual powers of each piece. The best way to learn is to play frequently and to study simple checkmates and endgame positions. This will rapidly give you a good idea of the strengths of the various pieces and help to develop an ability to calculate ahead. Do not lose a sense of proportion though. Regard defeats as experience and delight in the wins. Remember always, especially when having lost your queen, chess is only a game, to be played for fun and enjoyment!

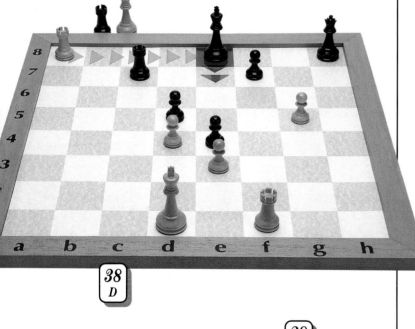

38 D

38 E

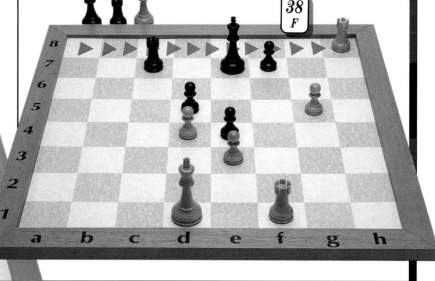

38 F

OPENINGS – HOW TO START A GAME

When starting a game it is important to understand the principles necessary to obtaining a good position in readiness for the battle ahead. This chapter outlines the general principles of opening play, and then introduces three popular opening sequences of moves so that you can understand the thinking that underlies the early development of your pieces.

GENERAL ADVICE

Develop your pieces onto squares where they will be most active. Development should take place quickly, and in general, continue until each piece is in play and the king has been castled.

The strategy of the opening is to try to control the center of the chess board. This is equivalent to an army obtaining the high ground ready to do battle from that vantage point.

Create the habit of examining your opponent's last move to check if a piece is under threat. Even if there is no direct threat, try to understand the purpose of and thinking behind the move. Then decide on a suitable response.

There are a number of popular openings that occur quite regularly where the moves follow a recognized pattern. These have names to identify how a game starts. Three recommended openings are the Spanish, the Queen's Gambit Declined, and the English. They are presented here with an explanation as to how they conform to opening principles.

THE SPANISH OR RUY LÓPEZ OPENING

This is one of the most famous openings in the whole of chess. It was recorded in a 1561 chess book written by Ruy López, a Spanish priest and the chess master at the court of King Philip II. The opening remains a favorite among Masters and Grandmasters, who, after decades of in-depth analysis, still find it provides a position from which winning chances and exciting games can be developed for either the Black or White side.

1. e4 A White pawn immediately occupies the center and opens lines for the queen and bishop to move out of the back rank.
...e5 Black does exactly the same (**1**).
2. Nf3 White brings a knight into play and threatens Black's central pawn.
...Nc6 Black responds by bringing his queen-side knight into play and protects his central pawn (**2**).
3. Bb5 This is the move that distinguishes the Spanish opening from others. The bishop threatens to take the knight which protects the central pawn.
...a6 Black chases the bishop away (**3**).

1

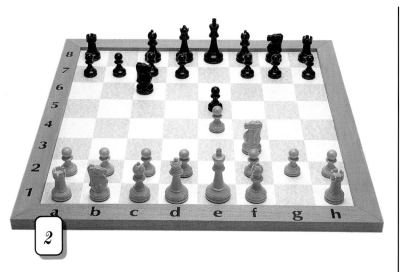

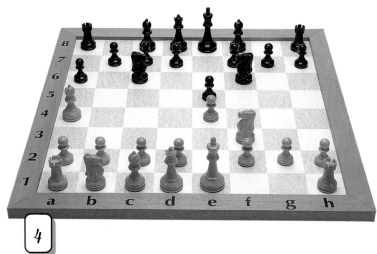

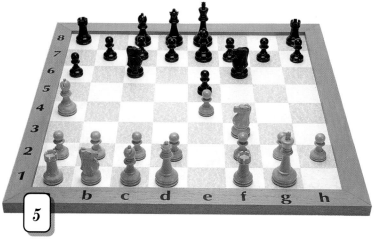

4. Ba4 The bishop maintains its threat as it keeps up indirect pressure on the center thus maintaining control.

...Nf6 Black responds by developing his other knight and threatens the White center pawn (**4**).

5. o-o This is an opening trap! If Black takes the White pawn, White will move his rook onto the king file and pin the knight and pawn against their king, creating complications that will be to White's advantage.

...Be7 Black's reply breaks the threatened pin, develops the bishop and prepares for castling (**5**).

6. c3 This pawn move prepares the way for a thrust in the center of the board.

...d6 while this pawn move strengthens the center ready for White's advance (**6**).

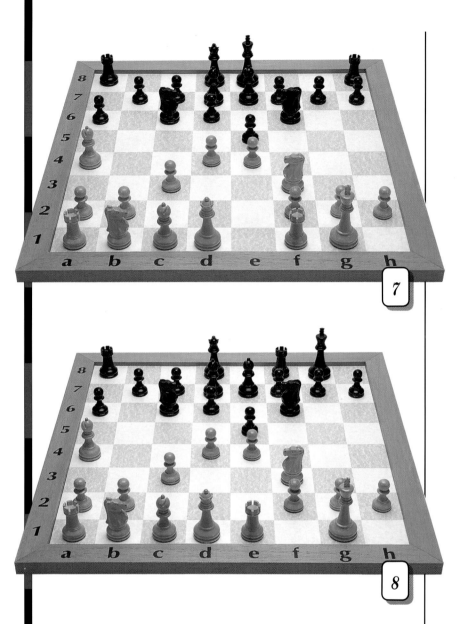

QUEEN'S GAMBIT DECLINED

Gambit is a chess term. It can refer to any opening which involves the planned sacrifice of material. The player hopes, in return, to obtain central control and/or rapid development of his pieces, which should create a promising attacking position. It derives from an Italian word meaning "to set a trap" or "trip up an opponent."

The Queen's Gambit Declined is an opening that goes back to the 15th century, but it is only in the 20th century with the introduction of international tournaments that it has become popular. With the Queen's pawn occupying the center, the game will produce an entirely different, more positional type of chess to the king-side openings.

This opening was played in the 1985 World Championship match between Anatoly Karpov (White) and Garry Kasparov (Black).

1. d4 The queen's pawn occupies a central square.
...d5 Black does the same (**9**).
2. Nf3 A knight is developed to cover the center.
...Nf6 Same (**10**).
3. c4 The queen's pawn is offered as a gambit. This is how the name of the opening came about.
...e6 The gambit is declined as Black provides extra cover to the central pawn (**11**).
4. Nc3 White develops the other knight toward the center.
...Be7 Black brings out a bishop and prepares to castle (**12**).
5. Bg5 The bishop comes out to an aggressive position.

7. d4 A central thrust.
...Bd7 Developing another piece and preparing a defense against the White pressure in the center (**7**).
8. Re1 Another piece improves its position and adds to the force aimed at the center.
...o-o Black castles the king into safety, preparing for the middle game battle (**8**).

White always has the advantage of the first move and this advantage has been maintained here. However, Black has been able to prepare a solid defense to counteract White's slight initiative. Both are now prepared for the battle ahead and the best player should win.

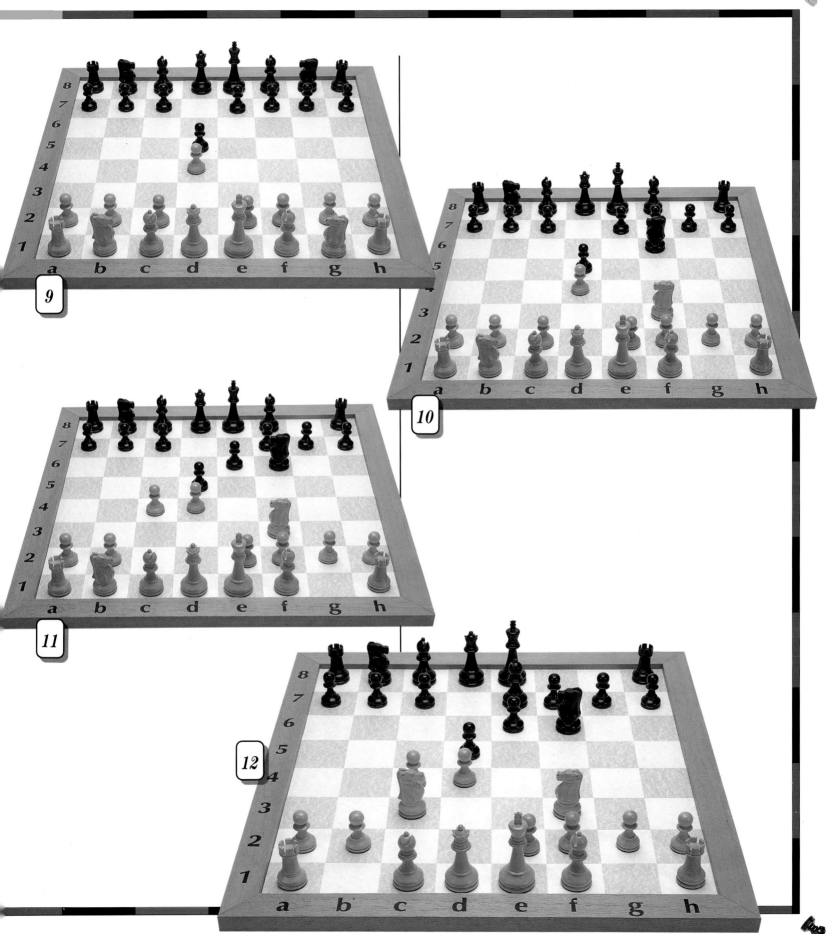

9

10

11

12

91

...h6 Black chases the bishop away (**13**).

6. Bh4 The bishop moves to the side of the board to maintain pressure along the diagonal.

...o-o Black castles, the king moves into a safer position and the rook is developed toward the center (**14**).

By move 14 the following position was reached (**15**). There has been an exchange of pawns in the center, all the minor pieces are developed, both sides have castled. This is a fairly even position. A number of exchanges starting with the White bishop taking the Black bishop followed, but neither player could obtain an advantage so by move 22 they agreed a draw.

THE ENGLISH OPENING

This is an opening used in a famous match played in 1843 between the English champion Howard Staunton and Frenchman Pierre Saint-Amant in Paris. Staunton played the opening six times in his impressive victory. In his chess magazine he wrote, "this opening may be adopted with perfect security." Since then it has often been used in world championship matches and its flexibility appeals to many of the present generation of young Grandmasters.

These moves follow a game played in 1994 between two of the finest young Grandmasters – "pretenders to the chess throne" – 18-year-old Vladimir Kramnic of Russia (White) and Viswanathan Anand, aged 25, from India (Black).

16

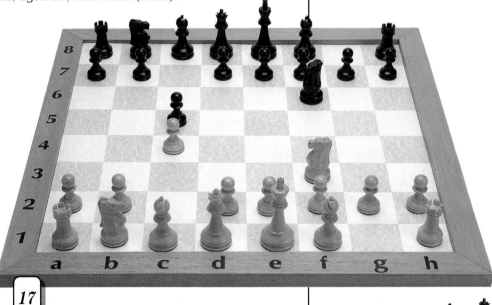

17

1. c4 White does not occupy the center but controls it with the queen's bishop pawn.
...c5 Black replies with a mirror move (**16**).
2. Nf3
...Nf6 The knights are developed with pressure on the center (**17**).
3. Nc3
...Nc6 All the knights are now on their best squares ready for action (**18**).

18

4. d4 White advances a pawn to a central square.

...cd It is immediately taken (**19**).

5. Nxp the pawn is recaptured and a knight is on a central square.

...e6 This pawn move prepares for a thrust in the center and opens the diagonal for a bishop (**20**).

6. g3 A move preparing for the bishop to move into the square vacated that will be followed by castling.

...Qb6 Developing the queen a little early to threaten the central knight (**21**).

7. Ndb5 An aggressive reply threatening to check the king on the queen's rank.

...Ne5 The knight move stops the threat and poses one by attacking the pawn on c4 (**22**).

8. Bg2 White ignores the threat and continues to develop his pieces and put extra pressure across the center.

...a6 Black hopes to drive away the knight from his aggressive outpost (**23**).

9. Qa4 Now if pxN the queen can take the rook.

...Neg4 However, this knight move threatens to win at once with queen taking the king's bishop pawn with check followed by the capture of the bishop (**24**).

The game went on to move 26 when it reached this position (**25**). (The intervening moves were: 10. o-o Rb8 11. b4! axb5 12. Nxb5 d5 13. Nd6+ Ke7 14. c5 Qa6 15. Qc2 Ne8 16. b5 Qa8 17. Bf4 Nxd6 18. Bxd6+ Ke8 19. Bxb8 QxB 20. a4 Qc7 21. Rfc1 f5 22. a5 Ne5 23. c6 b6 24. axb Qxb 25. Ra8 Kd8 26. Rb8 Anand resigns.

Study this position and enjoy trying to work out how Kramnic can win. There are a number of variations but they should soon lead to White winning more material, which at this high level of play will certainly lead to a win. Anand can see no effective counterplay, so he resigns.

19

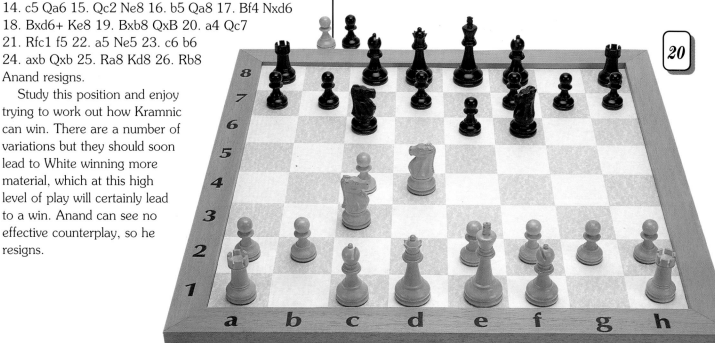

20

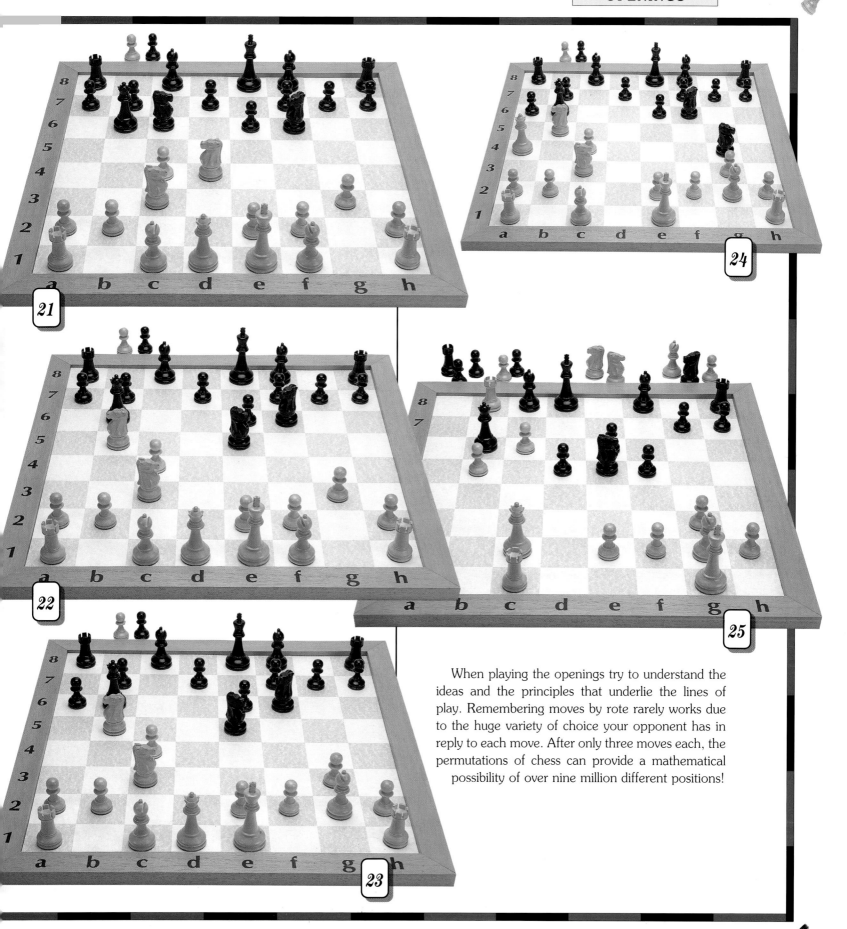

When playing the openings try to understand the ideas and the principles that underlie the lines of play. Remembering moves by rote rarely works due to the huge variety of choice your opponent has in reply to each move. After only three moves each, the permutations of chess can provide a mathematical possibility of over nine million different positions!

THE GREAT PLAYERS

Recorded chess positions have survived from the 9th century A.D. The historical record is part of the beauty of chess. It enables us to study, and learn from, the examples of the great players in chess history. This chapter introduces the "greats" in chess history. In Baghdad during the reign of Caliph al-Muktafi (902-908) a chess match was arranged between the court chess player al-Mawardi and his rival as-Suli (c.880-946). The match was won by as-Suli, who then replaced al-Mawardi as the Caliph's chess champion and went on to create a great reputation as a chess player that has lasted over the centuries. One of his endgame studies has only recently been solved with the aid of a computer.

RENAISSANCE MASTERS

The modern European game as we know it today was developed in Spain around 1475 when the powers of the queen and bishop were greatly increased, creating a more tactical game. Ruy López (c.1530-c.1580), a priest who was the court chess champion of Philip II, traveled to Italy in 1560 where he played and beat their leading players, Giovanni Leonardo and Paolo Boi. Some years later, in 1574, the Italians arranged a return match at the court of Philip II in Madrid. They both obtained their revenge by defeating Ruy López and were handsomely rewarded by the King. Royal patronage was common at this period. Many chess masters lived a comfortable life through being court entertainers with a similar status to minstrels and jesters.

Gioacchino Greco (c.1598-1634) from Calabria was the leading 17th century Italian master who made his living by traveling through Europe playing chess and selling his manuscripts of chess games to wealthy patrons. In France, in 1621, he succeeded in defeating three leading French players and winning a fortune of 5,000 crowns. Continuing his travels to England he was robbed en route to London and lost it all. However, he continued his practice of playing chess, together with preparing and selling his chess manuscripts to the nobility and so obtained a very lucrative living.

Above: The title page of Gioacchino Greco's 1707 French edition of *Le Jeu des Eschets*, The Game of Chess, dedicated to the Marquis de Louvois.

In 1624 he traveled to Spain where he met and defeated strong chess opponents at a tournament played at the court of Philip IV. He died in 1634 while on a trip to the Spanish West Indies. Many of Greco's manuscripts were a collection of games, possibly his own. Years after his death one of his French manuscripts was published and translated into several languages, repeated editions of which were still being issued two centuries later.

For one of his compositions he was awarded a pension of 25 *louis d'or* from the privy purse of King Louis XV. Unfortunately, because of this patronage, he was exiled from France during the time of the Revolution. He tragically died in London a few days before permission arrived for his return to France to rejoin his family.

Illustrated here is a position from Philidor's match against Count Bruhl, played in London in 1789. Philidor played White. This is the position after move 27 when Philidor, although in check, announced mate in two moves (**1**). The game continued 28. Qxf5 pxQf5 29. Rh8 mate (**2**).

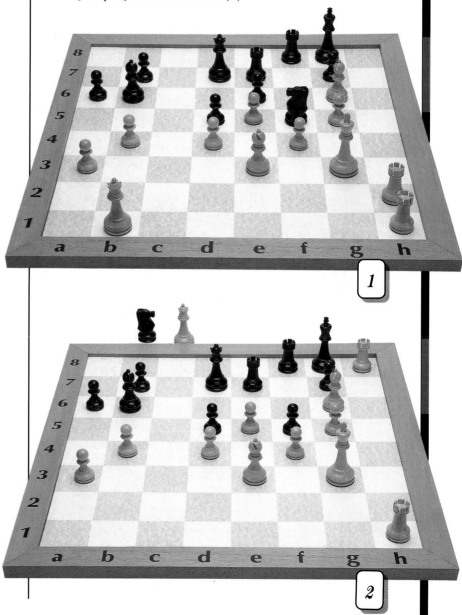

FRANÇOIS-ANDRÉ DANICAN PHILIDOR

In the 18th century, Paris became the international center of chess. Philidor (1726-95), who was equally talented as a musician and composer, was regarded as the best player. In 1747 he came to London and astounded everyone with his chess ability, comfortably beating the leading English players. In 1749 his *L'Analyze du Jeu des Échecs* (written in 1748) was published in London. This was an immediate success followed by translations into several languages, and resulting in over 100 versions being published during the next century.

He was loved for his chess by the English and for his music by the French. As a result he spent a part of each year, February to June, as a professional chess player at Parsloe's club, St. James, London returning to France to devote time to his music and his family for the remainder of the year. In 1782 he gave the first of his famous public blindfold displays. Usually this consisted of playing three games of chess simultaneously, two of them blindfolded – an astonishing feat at that time. His French friends were worried that the mental strain might cause him to go mad and advised him to give up chess and concentrate on his music. In Paris he regularly composed comic operas for the Opéra-Comique. He excelled at this, writing over twenty such works. One of his successes was the music for a production of *Tom Jones* first performed in 1765. He also composed music for grand opera and ballet.

Above: Philidor giving an exhibition of blindfold chess at Parsloe's Club in London in 1794. He played at Parsloe's for over 20 years.

HOWARD STAUNTON

Howard Staunton (1810-74) established himself as the world's leading chess player by decisively defeating the French champion, Pierre Charles Fournier de Saint-Amant, in 1843. This marked the end of French chess domination that had been maintained since the days of Philidor. For the rest of the 19th century London, and in particular a club called Simpson's Divan in the Strand, became the world's principal center for chess.

In 1847 Staunton confirmed his world position as Number One by winning matches against the Germans Horwitz and Harrwitz, the strongest players available at the time. Staunton energetically promoted chess, started England's first chess magazine, "*The Chess Player's Chronicle,*" and wrote an influential chess column in the "*Illustrated London News,*" dealing with over a hundred letters each week from interested readers. He published a number of authoritative books, including *The Chess Tournament*, (London 1852). This was an account of the world's first international tournament, organized by Staunton to coincide with the Great Exhibition held at the Crystal Palace in London's Hyde Park.

The tournament was won by German Adolf Anderssen, who also won his encounter against Staunton, thereby becoming unofficially the world's leading player. Staunton, however, still enjoyed immense prestige and continued promoting chess, although he retired from competitive matches, concentrating his energies on his literary work.

The standard chess sets used for all tournaments today carry Staunton's name. They had been designed by Nathaniel Cook, and manufactured by John Jaques & Son, who from 1849 sold the sets with Staunton's signature as an endorsement on the underside of each box.

Above: The label of the first Staunton pattern set sold in October, 1849.

The board illustrated (**3**) shows the position after move 24 in the match Staunton (White) v. Elijah Williams (Black) played in London in 1851. The game continued 25. Qd1! (threatening Qd4 and Qxg7 mate) Bc6 26. Bxc6 Qxc6 27. Qd4 Rf6 28. Rd6 Qb5 29. Rd8+ Rf8 30. Rxf8+ Kxf8 31. Qd6+ Ke8 32. Rd1 Resigns (33. Qd8 mate) (**4**).

Below: The Staunton v. Saint-Amant match played in Paris in 1843. Staunton's victory meant that London became the dominant center for chess for the rest of the century.

PAUL CHARLES MORPHY

Morphy (1837-84) was the first child to be recognized as a chess prodigy. Born in New Orleans, from the age of six he developed an exceptional talent playing with his father, Judge Alonzo Morphy, and his uncle Ernest. By the time he was eight he competed successfully with the strongest players in his home town of New Orleans and within a few years he succeeded in winning games against them all. In 1850 Janos Löwenthal, a world class chess master, visited New Orleans and was invited to Paul's home to assess his chess skill. They played three games and to Löwenthal's embarrassment young Paul Morphy won them all.

Paul initially followed the family tradition and studied law. He obtained the degree of LL.B. in 1857 when still too young to practice, but luckily his family's circumstances allowed him the time to pursue his amateur interest in chess. That same year the first American National Chess Congress was held in New York, providing the opportunity for Morphy to measure his skill against the strongest players in the United States. The result was sensational, Morphy won all his matches, and won with such imagination and style that new world America knew they had a champion to challenge old "stuck-up" Europe.

Morphy traveled to England the following year where he again impressed the chess community by winning matches against all the best players in London. He had challenged the retired Staunton, who seemed to accept his challenge but avoided fixing a date for such a match. Morphy moved on to Paris where a more important match was arranged against Europe's leading player, the German Adolf Anderssen from Breslau. Great interest was aroused as everyone realized that this match would decide who was the world's best chess player.

Above: Paul Morphy (left) playing against Jules Arnous de Rivière in Paris, 1858.

Above: Paul Morphy aged 22.

It was agreed the winner would be the first to win seven games. Anderssen won the first game, the second was drawn, then Morphy showed his genius by winning the next four, and only lost one more game before winning the match. It seemed inconceivable that a player of Anderssen's established ability could have been so decisively beaten. That was the achievement of this young man from New Orleans. He returned to a hero's welcome. Feted and honored in New York, Paul Morphy was the first American to obtain world supremacy in any sporting domain.

Morphy returned to New Orleans, but having satisfied himself and shown the world his chess talent, he declined to play any further competitive games. It had been his intention to play until he was 21, whereafter he meant to practice law. Chess, after all, was only a game. However, when he failed to establish himself as a lawyer, Morphy chose to live the quiet and idle life of a gentleman. He became increasingly withdrawn from society and suffered in later years from delusions of persecution. At the age of only 47 he died suddenly of a stroke while having a bath.

A NIGHT AT THE OPERA

In 1858 Paul Morphy played chess at the Paris Opéra, during a performance of *The Barber of Seville*, against the combined skills of the Duke of Brunswick and Count Isouard. The game shows Morphy at his best.

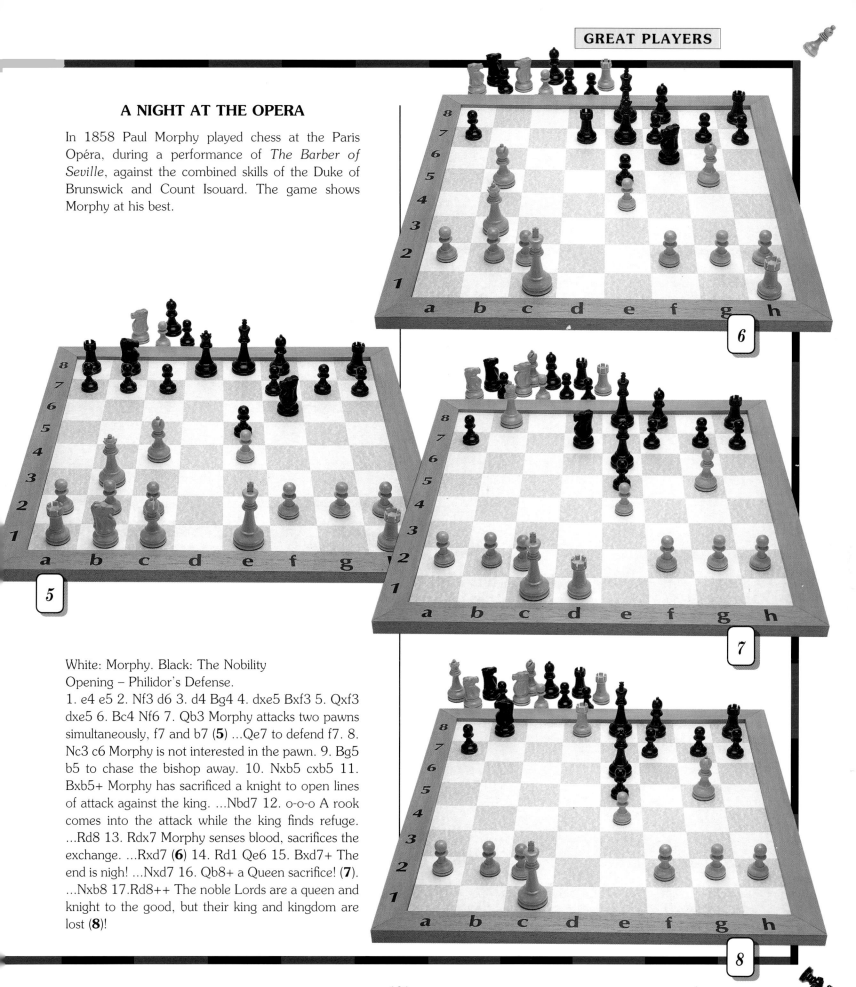

White: Morphy. Black: The Nobility
Opening – Philidor's Defense.
1. e4 e5 2. Nf3 d6 3. d4 Bg4 4. dxe5 Bxf3 5. Qxf3 dxe5 6. Bc4 Nf6 7. Qb3 Morphy attacks two pawns simultaneously, f7 and b7 (**5**) ...Qe7 to defend f7. 8. Nc3 c6 Morphy is not interested in the pawn. 9. Bg5 b5 to chase the bishop away. 10. Nxb5 cxb5 11. Bxb5+ Morphy has sacrificed a knight to open lines of attack against the king. ...Nbd7 12. o-o-o A rook comes into the attack while the king finds refuge. ...Rd8 13. Rdx7 Morphy senses blood, sacrifices the exchange. ...Rxd7 (**6**) 14. Rd1 Qe6 15. Bxd7+ The end is nigh! ...Nxd7 16. Qb8+ a Queen sacrifice! (**7**). ...Nxb8 17.Rd8++ The noble Lords are a queen and knight to the good, but their king and kingdom are lost (**8**)!

WILHELM STEINITZ, WORLD CHAMPION 1886-1894

Wilhelm Steinitz (1836-1900) was born in Prague, went to Vienna as a young man, then moved to London in 1862 where he established himself as a strong chess master, winning matches against the best English and foreign masters, and becoming a powerful professional chess player. During 1866 he played and won an important match against Adolf Anderssen, winner of the 1851 and 1862 London International Tournaments. After this win Steinitz dominated chess in Europe, winning tournaments in London 1872, and Vienna 1873.

However, Johann Zukertort's outstanding success in the London 1883 Tournament caused many chess players to claim Zukertort as the world's leading player. To decide which of these two dominant chess personalities was the better player, the first chess match for the official title of "World Champion" was arranged. This took place in 1886, in three separate venues. The first was New York; the players then moved to St. Louis for the second stage, and finished at New Orleans. Steinitz, after losing the first four games, made a remarkable recovery, to eventually win by ten games to five with five drawn. He was the first player to be recognized, by popular acclaim, as an official World Champion. Zukertort never understood how he lost. He became unwell and was never fully to recover his health, dying two years later in London from a stroke.

Steinitz emigrated to the United States, eventually becoming an American citizen. The title "World Champion" was established as Steinitz's personal property. The champion had the right to select his own challengers, but this tended to restrict the championship to those who could raise sufficient funds to offer as stake money, and on occasions the strongest challenger could be avoided. Steinitz successfully defended the title twice against the Russian Master Mikhail Chigorin in 1889 and 1892.

In 1894 Steinitz confidently allowed the young Emanuel Lasker, who had not won any major tournaments, but who could find the stake money, to play a match for his world championship title. Unexpectedly Steinitz lost, and he failed to recover the title in a return match. The strain of this second

match, played in Moscow, causd Steinitz to have a mental breakdown.

The ex-World Champion had to spend some time in a mental institution, where he believed he could play God, giving him odds of pawn and move. For a while he recovered and continued to play in the strongest international tournaments. However Steinitz was again taken seriously ill in 1900, dying in New York, penniless. He is buried in Green-Lawn Cemetery, Brooklyn, where a commemorative granite stone, engraved wth a chess board, honors the memory of the first Chess Champion of the World.

The position illustrated (**9**) comes from the match between A. Meitner (White) and Steinitz (Black) played in Vienna in 1882. From this position Steinitz (playing blindfold) checkmated in three moves: ...Rh1+ 2. Bxh1 Qxf2+ 3. Bg2 Qg1 mate (**10**).

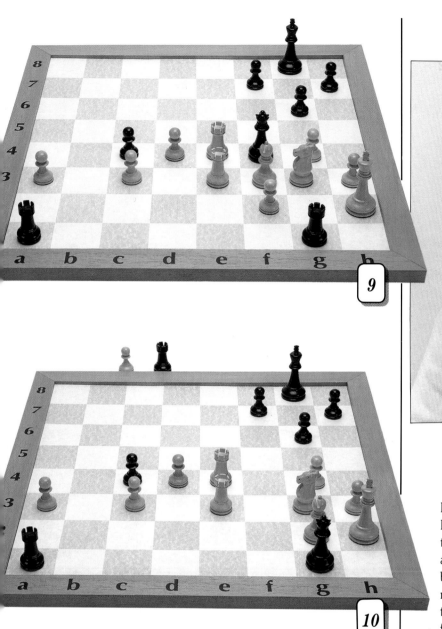

EMANUEL LASKER,
WORLD CHAMPION 1894-1921

Emanuel Lasker (1868-1941) was born in Berlinchen, Germany (but now Barlinek in Poland), the son of the cantor of the local synagogue. At the age of eleven Emanuel was sent to live with his elder brother Berthold, who was in Berlin to study medicine. However, when their father discovered that his sons were spending their time playing chess for stakes in a local tearoom, he immediately transferred his son Emanuel to a school in Landsburg.

Here he showed a remarkable talent for mathematics, and within a few years he was back in Berlin to study at the university. In 1889 Lasker decided to abandon his studies temporarily to devote time to chess. He entered and won a German candidate's tournament, thereby obtaining his Master's title. The major international tournament was won by Dr. Siegbert Tarrasch who, because of his consistent tournament successes, was regarded in Europe as the next champion of the world.

Lasker played and won a number of small tournaments in Germany, Austria, and England before moving to the United States. From the States, he tried to arrange a match with Dr. Tarrasch, but was refused in such an arrogant manner that Lasker responded by directly challenging the World Champion, Wilheim Steinitz. Steinitz had successfully defended his title on numerous occasions since his victory against Zukertort. By accepting the challenge from the young, relatively inexperienced Lasker, Steinitz reckoned that he could delay playing a match against his main challenger, Dr. Tarrasch, for a while longer.

The match was played in May 1894. Emanuel Lasker won convincingly by ten wins to five losses with four draws to become the second chess champion of the world. However, he still had to prove to the chess fraternity in general, and Dr. Tarrasch in particular, that he was worthy of his new status. Lasker did this in style, winning four successive major tournaments: St. Petersburg 1895/6, Nuremberg 1896, London 1899, and Paris 1900.

In 1902 he took time off from chess to obtain a doctorate in mathematics at Erlangen University. A number of years were to pass before the match that

the chess public desired was arranged – Dr. Emanuel Lasker v. Dr. Siegbert Tarrasch. It took place in two German cities, Munich and Düsseldorf, during the months of August and September 1908. The negotiations for the match were protracted and acrimonious; there had been bad feeling between them since Tarrasch had refused Lasker's challenge in 1894. Before the start of the first game, Tarrasch refused to shake hands, saying "To you, Herr Lasker, I have only these words to say: Check and Mate."

The match began in this hostile atmosphere and became worse when Tarrasch lost the first two games. By the eleventh game Lasker led by seven wins to two losses, and the end came in the sixteenth game when Tarrasch blundered in time pressure. The final score was eight wins to three losses and five draws. Dr. Emanuel Lasker went on to win many further challenges, eventually retaining the world title for 27 years, the longest tenure of any champion.

Our board (**11**) comes from a game that Lasker (White) played against Fritz Englund (Black) in Scheveningen in 1913. From this even-looking position, Lasker checkmated in two moves. 1. Qxc6+ Pxc6 2. Ba6 checkmate (**12**).

JOSÉ RAUL CAPABLANCA, WORLD CHAMPION 1921-27

José Raul Capablanca (1888-1942) was born in Cuba. A child prodigy, he learned chess at the age of four. By the time he was thirteen he had defeated the Cuban champion in an informal match by four games to three with six draws.

Above: "Oo won Guv'nor?" "I regret to say that Capablanca was beaten at the 43rd move." (from the humorous magazine "*Punch*").

Capablanca went to New York to be educated in 1904. There he joined the Manhattan Chess Club and rapidly gained experience against strong oppositon, including the World Champion, Emanuel Lasker. By 1911 he had proved, with an impressive string of tournament successes, that he was the natural challenger for Lasker's title. Negotiation became protracted, and was further delayed by the intervention of World War I. It was 1921 before Capablanca and Lasker sat down to face one another over the board as rivals in a title match.

The games took place in Havana, Cuba for a record stake of $25,000. Capablanca won, four games to nil, ten games being drawn. This was the most decisive result by any challenger to the world championship. Capablanca became an international

celebrity, universally admired while living the life of a playboy. At chess he was regarded as invincible; he was at the peak of his powers. Tournament results were: first in London 1922, second in New York 1924, and in 1927 his greatest tournament triumph, first in New York easily ahead of Alekhine, and all the others. His losses became so rare that on one occasion the front page headline of the *New York Times* read "Capablanca Loses."

To practically everybody's surprise, in the same year, 1927, he lost the world title to Alexander Alekhine at Buenos Aires. He was unable to obtain a return match, but continued to achieve outstanding results on the tournament circuit: first at Ramsgate, Barcelona and Budapest in 1929, first in Moscow and Nottingham in 1936.

Capablanca was taken seriously ill during a 1938 tournament in Holland, and for the first time, finished well down the table. His health became a cause for concern. Also, the outbreak of World War II in Europe in 1939 restricted the organizing of international chess events. Capablanca was playing chess at the Manhattan Chess Club, New York, on March 8, 1942, when he had a heart attack and died. Alexander Alekhine wrote: "With his death, we have lost a very great chess genius whose like we shall never see again."

13

14

ALEXANDER ALEKHINE, WORLD CHAMPION 1927-35 AND 1937-46

Alexander Alekhine (1892-1946) was the first Russian world champion. He was the son of wealthy aristocratic parents, his father being a member of the last parliament of the Tsars. Alekhine obtained his chess Master title in 1910 and by 1914 was threatening the supremacy of Lasker and Capablanca. When World War I broke out Alekhine was leading in an international tournament in Mannheim. The tournament was stopped and the Russian players interned as prisoners of war. Alekhine somehow managed to negotiate his release and returned to Russia where he served in the equivalent of the Red Cross, but still finding time in 1915 and 1916 to win the Moscow Championship.

The position illustrated (**13**) is from a match played between Ossip Bernstein (White) and Capablanca (Black) in Moscow in 1914. Black's brilliant move at 29 (Qb2) seems to be a blunder until White tries to take the queen. The only reasonable move is to resign.

The possible variations are remarkable. (A) 1. Qxb2 Rd1 mate. (B) 1. Rc8 Qa1+ 2. Qf1 Qxf1+ 3. Kxf1 Rxc8 (wins rook). (C) 1. Rc2 Qb1+ 2. Qf1 Qxc2 (wins rook). (D) 1. Qe1 Qxc3 2. Qxc3 Rd1+ 3. Qe1 Rxe1 checkmate (**14**).

During the Russian Revolution that followed Alekhine was not only deprived of his family fortunes, but had to consider the safety of his life due to his aristocratic origins. Ironically when the Ukraine was liberated in 1919, he was imprisoned in a death cell charged with "links with White Russian counter-intelligence." Again Alekhine survived and a year later he joined the Communist Party and went on to win the first Soviet Chess Championship. From 1921 to 1927 he gained first place in eight international tournaments and with these victories he established his right to play Capablanca for the World Championship.

This match was Cabablanca's first defense of the title, played in 1927 in Buenos Aires for a stake of $10,000. Alekhine prepared by studying every game that his invincible opponent had played, determined to find some weakness in his play. Capablanca, who had never lost a game to Alekhine, relied entirely on his mammoth natural talent. He never felt the need to prepare for any match.

Alekhine's determination and industry provided the reward he desired, winning the prolonged match by six games to three losses and 25 draws. Alekhine defended his title on a number of occasions, but never again against Capablanca, who tried in vain to negotiate a return match. During World War II, Alekhine who was resident in France, played in a number of Nazi-organized tournaments in occupied Europe, including some in Germany.

In 1941 a series of outrageously anti-semitic articles, attributed to Alekhine, were published, titled *"Jewish and Aryan Chess."* These articles threatened to ruin his reputation and career. Finally, in 1946 in a hotel room in Estoril, Portugal, he unexpectedly died of a heart attack.

The position shown (**15**) arose in a match between Alekhine (White) and Aron Nimzowitsch (Black) played in Bled in Yugoslavia in 1931. From this position Alekhine methodically destroys Black. 1. Bh5 Nxh5 2. Rd8+ Kf7 3. Qxh6 Resigns. Nimzowitsch could see ... Kg7 4. Nxe4 Pxe4 5. Bh6+ (**16**) allowing Alekhine's queen to capture the Black queen.

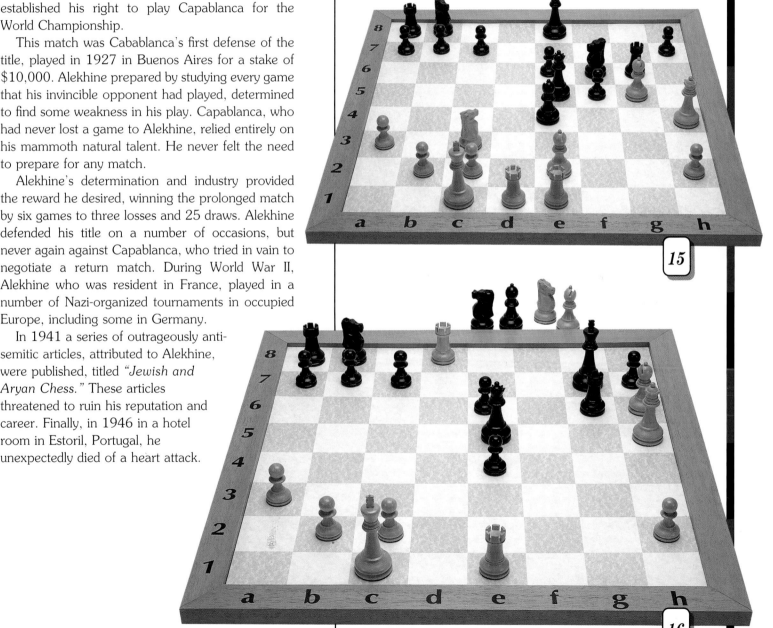

15

16

DR. MACHGIELIS (MAX) EUWE, WORLD CHAMPION 1935-7

Dutchman Max Euwe (1901-81) was born in Watergrafsmeer, near Amsterdam. Euwe was a highly gifted chess player who managed to remain an amateur throughout his life. A doctor and teacher of mathematics, chess always took second place to his profession. However, his natural abilities propelled him to the pinnacle of chess achievement. In the thirties Euwe had several outstanding tournaments, obtaining a number of first places ahead of Capablanca, Alekhine, and the young Russian Mikhail Botvinnik.

By 1935 he had earned the right to play Alekhine for the World Championship. The match was played in the Netherlands and after a close and gruelling

Below: Max Euwe is seen standing behind Mikhail Botvinnik on the occasion of the 11th Chess Olympics which took place in Amsterdam in 1954.

Right: Max Euwe defeated Alekhine for the World Championship in 1935. He went on to become a very active President of FIDE in the period 1970-1978.

encounter Max Euwe became the only Dutchman so far to be crowned World Champion. In Amsterdam his achievements have been permanently honored by the naming of a shopping and office development as the "Max Euwe Center". As the result of his experience with Capablanca, Alekhine made sure that he had a return match clause included in the contract and this return match took place in Holland in 1937. Alekhine, smarting from his earlier defeat, prepared properly – even giving up drink for the duration of the match – and retrieved his title with a resounding victory.

Max Euwe wrote more chess books than any other great player. He was also involved with the early research into chess computer programming, and was actively concerned with chess administration. In 1970 he was elected President of FIDE (the World Chess Federation).

THE SOVIET DOMINATION

After the death of Alekhine the International Chess Federation (FIDE – Fédération Internationale des Échecs) took control of the world title. They organized a tournament between the leading contenders: Euwe, Reshevsky, Botvinnik, Smyslov and Keres (Lasker and Capablanca had died during the war years). The winner would be declared the official World Champion. The tournament took place in 1948, the first half played at the Hague and the completion in Moscow. The Soviet Union had decided to promote chess as an example of the benefits of living under Commmunist ideology.

Mikhail Botvinnik, born near St. Petersburg in 1911, was the favourite to win the tournament, and this he did decisively, winning ten games and only losing two, with eight draws. Botvinnik was the ideal champion for the U.S.S.R. – he believed in the ideals of Communism, remained a genuine amateur, obtained his doctorate in science and achieved international distinction as an electrical engineer.

Under the new rules the World Champion had to defend his title every three years against an opponent who qualified by winning a candidates' tournament. In 1951 and 1954 Botvinnik drew against his challengers, David Bronstein and Vasily Smyslov, both times retaining his title in accordance with the rules. In 1957 he was defeated by Smyslov, only to regain the championship in the return match in 1958.

He lost the World Championship again in 1960 to Mikhail Tal (1936-93), a most exciting young talent who electrified the chess world with his uninhibited attacking play. But Botvinnik had only loaned him his title, again winning the return match. In 1963 it was the Armenian Tigran Petrosian who met and defeated Botvinnik. This time however, the

Above: Botvinnik, Smyslov and Paul Keres, one of the best players not to win the title.

Above: Botvinnik won the title three times.

return match privilege was abolished. Botvinnik, aged 53, retired from competitive chess.

Petrosian (1929-84), the new World Champion, had a negative, defensive style of play that made him very difficult to defeat. Petrosian defended his world title twice, in 1966 and 1969. Both times the challenger was Boris Spassky (b.1937). Petrosian won the first match but had to concede the title to Spassky in 1969. Spassky was a very popular champion, easily approachable, a man who had a pleasant personality and played attractive imaginative chess.

Above: The world title match in 1963. Tigran Petrosian defeated Botvinnik to become World Champion for the next six years.

Ever since Botvinnik had won the championship in 1948, the Soviets had dominated the chess scene. All the champions and challengers were from the well-organized, state-sponsored, Soviet school of chess. However, this was about to change.

Above: The extraordinary Bobby Fischer.

BOBBY FISCHER, WORLD CHAMPION 1972-5

The domination of the world chess championship by players reared under the Communist system was interrupted by a unique product from capitalist America. Robert James (Bobby) Fischer (b.1943) was brought up in Brooklyn, learning chess from his sister at the age of six. He became completely absorbed by the game, dedicating his whole being to obtaining excellence over the board. At 14 he won the junior and senior championships of the U.S.A.

Fischer became obsessed with the ambition to win the World Championship. He impressed the whole chess fraternity with his outstanding talent by winning numerous international tournaments. Initially, his ambitions were thwarted by the strongest of the Soviet Grandmasters. In the final stages of a World Championship cycle they would outscore him. In his frustration he accused them of cheating, playing as a team in order to prevent his success.

The rules were changed to meet Fischer's objection: in 1971 the candidates' finals were played in a series of knock-out matches. Fischer obtained an astonishing result in the first match against Russian Grandmaster Mark Taimanov, winning all six games. The second match was even more amazing as he did exactly the same against Danish Grandmaster Bent Larsen, another six-nothing result. At this level of chess, between the world's leading Grandmasters, these results should be impossible, yet Bobby Fischer achieved the impossible - *twice*. The final hurdle towards the World Championship match was against the previous champion Tigran Petrosian, probably the best defensive player ever.

This match was to be decided by the best of twelve games. The first game showed that Petrosian had prepared well for the encounter. He obtained the advantage from the opening, only to go astray and allow Fischer to continue his remarkable run of victories. The second game saw the experienced Soviet player launch a magnificent attack, make no mistakes and leave our American hero completely lost. The magic was over, reality had returned. Bobby Fischer was badly shaken. He was lucky to maintain the status-quo during the next three games. Petrosian seemed to be in control. Then, in the sixth game, he played badly, allowing Fischer to win. With his confidence restored, Bobby dominated the rest of the match eventually winning six and a half to two and a half.

MATCH OF THE CENTURY

The "Match of the Century," as the World Championship was proclaimed by the international press, was to be more dramatic off the board than on it. It was to be an intellectual war of ideologies – Capitalism v. Communism. Never has a chess match

received so much media coverage. Fischer, having obtained his goal, was emotionally terrified. He made all kinds of irrational demands of the Icelandic organizers, even risking his life's ambition by not appearing on the official starting date to face the World Champion, popular, calm, and affable Boris Spassky. To the relief of everyone, Bobby Fischer did eventually appear, after the receipt of a pleading letter from the American Secretary of State, Henry Kissinger, and an extra £50,000 in prize money from British financier Jim Slater. The match was rescheduled to start on July 11, 1972.

The first game was won by Spassky. Fischer complained that the television cameras were disturbing his concentration and demanded that they be removed. He refused to play the second game when he saw the cameras were still in place. The game was awarded to Spassky. Two-nil. It seemed that the match would be abandoned and many reporters and spectators left Reykjavik convinced there would be no further play. However, Spassky, determined that the match should continue, agreed to Fischer's irrational demand that he would only play the third game if it were in a private room, without spectators or cameras.

The game was a masterpiece; the turning point of the match and Fischer's first-ever win against Boris Spassky. The major positions are illustrated overleaf. For the fourth game, the contestants moved back onto the stage, but with no cameras. The match continued with Fischer now outplaying Spassky. By the sixth game he took the lead, eventually winning the match by four clear points. Statistically, the new World Champion was also the strongest player in the recorded history of the game.

Having climbed his Everest, Fischer, to the frustration of all chess lovers, withdrew from serious play. For the 1975 World Championship match Bobby Fischer demanded numerous changes to the conditions of play. On learning that they were not totally acceptable, he immediately sent a telegram ending with the words "I therefore resign my World Championship title." This allowed the new challenger, Anatoly Karpov, to become the World Chess Champion by default.

Left: 1972 – the American eagle swoops to steal the crown from the Russian bear.

THE THIRD MATCH GAME, REYKJAVIK 1972

This game was played in a private room behind the stage, watched in the Exhibition Hall on closed-circuit television. Only a handful of chess enthusiasts had come to the hall, hoping for a last minute miracle. This was the outcome, for which they can be eternally grateful. They can say – "We were there."

Spassky (White) v. Fischer (Black).

Opening – Modern Benoni.

1. d4 Nf6	2. c4 e6
3. Nf3 c5	4. d5 exd5
5. cxd5 d6 (**17**)	

Fischer chooses a sharp opening, allowing White a pawn majority in the center, on which he intends to apply pressure.

	6. Nc3 g6
7. Nd2 Nbd7	8. e4 Bg7
9. Be2 o-o	

They both castle, the kings are safe.

	10. o-o Re8 (**18**)

Rooks centralized.

11. Qc2 Nh5	12. Bxh5 gxh5

Spassky exchanges his bishop for the knight as he also weakens the Black defense around the king.

13. Nc4 Ne5	14. Ne3 Qh4
15. Bd2 Ng4! (**19**)	

Black is suddenly attacking, threatening mate on the next move.

	16. Nxg4 hxg4
17. Bf4 Qf6	

Attacking the bishop.

	18. g3 Bd7

Develops the last piece and connects the rooks.

19. a4 b6	20. Rfe1 a6

Both players are quietly maneuvering, Black to advance on the queen-side, White in the center.

21. Re2 b5	22. Rae1 Qg6

To stop e5.

23. b3 Re7	24. Qd3 Rb8
25. axb5 axb5	26. b4 c4 (**20**)

Black has created a strong passed pawn.

27. Qd2 Rbe8	28. Re3 h5
29. R3e2 Kh7	30. Re3 Kg8
31. R3e2 Bxc3	

Fischer now wins a pawn.

	32. Qxc3 Rxe4
33. Rxe4 Rxe4	34. Rxe4 Qxe4 (**21**)

Spassky knows he is losing but hopes for some drawing chances as remaining bishops move on opposite colored squares

35. Bh6 Qg6

White threatened mate.

36. Bc1 Qb1

Pinning the bishop against the king.

37. Kf1 Bf5	38. Ke2 Qe4+
39. Qe3 Qc2+	40. Qd2 Qb3
41. Qd4 Bd3+ (**22**)	

Spassky resigns, after 42. Ke3 Qd1 43. Bb2 (threatening mate) Qf3+ 44. Kd2 Qe2+ 45. Kc1 Qc2 mate (**23**).

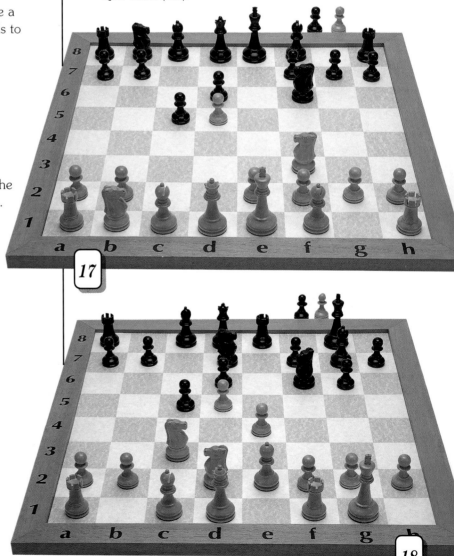

Above: Mind power wins the game.

113

ANATOLY KARPOV, WORLD CHAMPION 1975-85

With Bobby Fischer in self-imposed exile from the chess scene, the Soviet domination was reasserted. The new champion Anatoly Karpov (b.1951) was more frustrated than anyone with Fischer's decision. Even an offer of $5 million to hold the match in the Philippines could not tempt Fischer to play. Karpov felt he had to prove that he was worthy of the title so easily obtained. This he proceeded to do, obtaining seven first tournament prizes in 1975/76. He defeated Viktor Korchnoi in his first defense of the world title in 1978, and again three years later.

Karpov continued to dominate the international tournament circuit, his successes surpassing those of any other player. After a decade as World Champion in 1984, a new challenger to Karpov arrived in the form of the ambitious, hugely gifted, and confident twenty-one-year-old, Garry Kasparov. The first to win six games would be World Champion. Kasparov, overeager to demonstrate his natural chess genius, found instead that he was receiving a lesson from an experienced champion. Karpov was soon leading by four wins to nil.

There followed seventeen draws before Karpov won a fifth game, leaving him only one short of retaining the title. Kasparov, completely against his character, continued his patient drawing tactics, slowly exhausting the champion. After a further 21 games when the score of this (now) embarrassing marathon match stood at five wins to Karpov, three to Kasparov, the President of the World Chess Federation, Florencio Campomanes, stopped the encounter on the grounds that both players were exhausted.

A new match was arranged for the following year. Kasparov, having learned from their first match how best to play Karpov, won by two clear points. Garry Kasparov, aged twenty-two, became the youngest ever World Chess Champion.

To appreciate Karpov at his best, study this position (**24**) which occurred in a match played in Leningrad in 1986, again against Garry Kasparov. Kasparov (Black) resigned in this position as he can see no way to stop Karpov forcing the pass pawn on c6 to the eighth rank and promoting. A possible sequence is ...Rd8 2. Rxd4 Rxd4 3. Pc7 Rc8 4. Rb8 Rxb8 5. Pxb8+ (**25**).

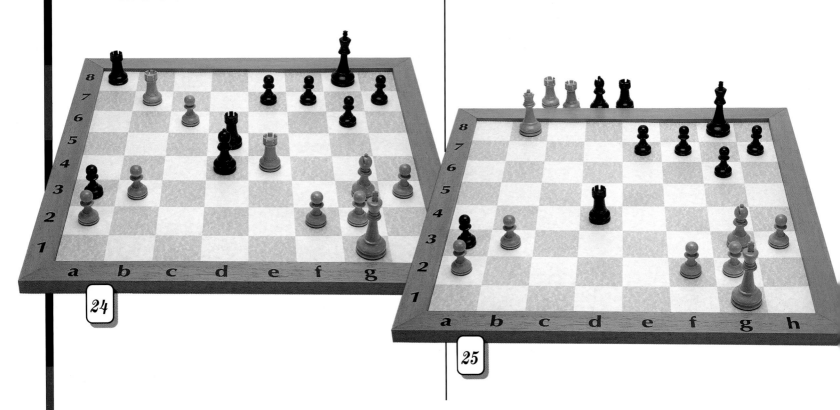

114

losing the final game to allow Kasparov to draw the match and thereby retain the title.

To see Kasparov in action, look at board (**26**). It is taken from a game between Kasparov (White) and the Hungarian Grandmaster Laslo Portisch in Niksic in 1983. In this position Kasparov played 1. Bxg7!! starting an imaginative attack. This is how play developed ...Kxg7 2. Ne5! Rfd8 3. Qg4+ Kf8 4. Qf5 f6 5. Nd7+ Rxd7 6. Rxd7 Qc5 7. Qh7 Rc7 8. Qh8+ Kf7 9. Rd3 Nc4 10. Rfd1! Ne5? 11. Qh7+ Ke6 12. Qg8+ Kf5 13. g4+ Kf4 14. Rd4+! Kf3 15. Qb3+ Qc3 16. Qd5+ (**27**). Wins.

Above: Karpov (left) and Kasparov have contested the title four times in a decade.

GARRY KASPAROV, WORLD CHAMPION 1985-

Garry Kasparov was born in the Azerbaijani town of Baku on the Black Sea on April 13, 1963. He was originally named Harry Weinstein. When his father died, while he was still a child, his family chose to use his mother's maiden name, Kasparov, and outside the U.S.S.R., his first name was pronounced as Garry. So Garry Kasparov he became. It was soon obvious that he had an immense natural talent for chess. Kasparov combined this talent with a disciplined zeal, dedicated to obtaining chess perfection, and driven by an ardent ambition to be the world's best-ever chess master.

In 1980, on his seventeenth birthday, he obtained his Grandmaster title, and later the same year he won the World Junior Championship (U.21). Kasparov's tournament successes for the next few years placed him at the top of the world ranking list.

In 1984 he qualified to play Karpov for the World Championship title by defeating past World Champion, Vasily Smyslov, in the candidates' final by four wins to nine draws. How he came to beat Karpov and take the title has already been described in the entry on Karpov.

Since the 1984 World Championship match the "two K's" have continued to dominate competitive chess. They contested the next three title matches, Kasparov retaining his title by narrow victories. In 1987 the match was drawn, Karpov, unbelievably,

RECENT DEVELOPMENTS

In 1993 English Grandmaster Nigel Short split the domination of the two K's by brilliantly defeating Karpov in the semi-final candidates' match, and winning the final against Grandmaster Jan Timman, so qualifying to meet Kasparov. However, before their match took place, both Kasparov and Short were furious at what they believed to be the inept attempts of the World Chess Federation (FIDE) to obtain the best sponsorship for their match. They split from FIDE, created a new breakaway organization, the "Professional Chess Association," and accepted an offer of £1,700,000 as prize money from sponsors *The Times* newspaper. The venue for the Championship match was the Savoy Theatre in London.

The World Chess Federation retaliated, claiming the World Championship title as their property. They organized their own match between past-champion Anatoly Karpov and Jan Timman.

To add confusion to confusion, Bobby Fischer decided, after twenty years, to come out of retirement and played a return match against Boris Spassky in Belgrade, Serbia, for his World Championship Title, pointing out that as he had never been defeated, he was still the proper Chess Champion of the World.

The results were: Kasparov defeated Short. Karpov won against Timman. Fischer beat Spassky. The present situation therefore is:
- Professional Chess Association World Champion – Garry Kasparov
- FIDE World Chess Federation World Champion – Anatoly Karpov
- Robert James Fischer World Champion – Robert (Bobby) Fischer.

Above: Bobby Fischer (right) playing Boris Spassky in the rematch for the "world title" that was held in Yugoslavia in 1992. Fischer won again.

Right: Nigel Short who challenged Garry Kasparov for a breakaway version of the world title. In the event he was comprehensively beaten.

CHESS – THE PEOPLE'S GAME

A few years ago a survey showed that over three million people played chess in Britain. Of these, about two million nine hundred and ninety thousand play casual, friendly chess. There are also many thousands who enjoy playing serious competitive chess. Similar percentage figures would apply in the United States, France or Germany. Only in the countries of the former U.S.S.R., where chess has been promoted by the state, would the proportion of players competing in tournaments be significantly larger, but even there, they would be grossly outnumbered by those who play for pure social enjoyment.

Right: Citizens of Washington D.C. enjoy a spring day by playing chess in a park near the White House.

Below: In the same park, a charming bronze statue commemorates the social side of the peoples' game, chess.

Above: "A Game at Chess" 1832, here between King William IV and Prime Minister Lord Gray.

A POPULAR PASTIME

The game is a people's game. This can be seen every day, across the globe, in the city squares and parks of Moscow, Berlin, Paris, London and New York (to mention a few). Everywhere people can be seen enjoying a game of chess during their leisure periods. In the 24-hour-city, New York, chess devotees play in the many coffee houses of Greenwich Village, and in Washington Square Park, where chess tables are provided. Crowds gather daily to play and watch the games in progress. Occasionally, celebrities like Kim Novak, the movie actress, or ex-world heavyweight

boxing champion Lennox Lewis might be spotted among the participants. The ready availability of portable or pocket chess sets – items which have been around for many years now – means that chess can be played on the move, wherever you are. It is a game for all occasions.

CHESS VARIANTS

Postal, telephone, or fax chess is an interesting form of the game, particularly for those who work unsocial hours, or possibly live in isolated areas. There is more time to consider each move, even to obtain assistance. The advent of computers has also extended the way in which chess can be played. Rather than taking on a human opponent, you can pit your wits against a machine.

COMPUTER CHESS

The first chess automaton was a very clever illusion. Invented in 1769 by Baron Wolfgang von Kempelen to entertain Empress Maria Theresa at the Imperial Court of Austria, "The Turk" (as von Kempelen named his invention) was a life-size figure in Turkish dress, seated behind a desk-shaped cabinet inlaid with a chess board. The cabinet was first displayed with all doors open, dispelling the thought that a person could be inside operating it. The automaton amazed everyone by appearing able to play chess against human opponents. The illusion was so successful that for over 80 years it toured through Europe and the United States to packed theaters. Among the many famous opponents of the Turk were Benjamin Franklin and Emperor Napoleon Bonaparte. In fact, the machine was an illusion. A small player was concealed inside who operated the Turk's arms to move the pieces.

It is only relatively recently that marketable chess-playing computers have been available. In the 1970s the most powerful of computers, which cost millions to develop, could not win a match against a chess Master. In 1994 at the Intel World Chess Speed Tournament in London, World Champion Garry Kasparov lost a game in the first round to a computer program that cost a few hundred dollars. However, Garry Kasparov remains the World Chess Champion, and it will be a few years yet, if ever, before a computer, under strict tournament conditions, will claim that title.

For most chess players the computer is an excellent companion. It can be adapted to play at any suitable strength, is always available to play, has no personality defects, and can be fixed, when you are in the mood, to lose a game without loss of face. A perfect opponent, it may in the future become the most popular form of chess play.

Left: Baron von Kempelen's chess automaton "The Turk," which was first displayed in 1770 at the court of the Empress Maria Theresa of Austria.

Right: Anatoly Karpov gives a demonstration of simultaneous chess during the 1990 congress of Chess Collectors International.

SIMULTANEOUS DISPLAY

Simultaneous displays are usually organized as entertainment at major chess events. They normally consist of 20 to 40 opponents being played at the same time by a chess master. The master moves from table to table inside a large circle, while his competition sit on the outside. Each player must make a move when the chess master arrives at his board. For special occasions, marathon simultaneous displays have been organized. In 1984 Czech Grandmaster Vlastimil Hort played 663 games over 33 hours, obtaining an 80 percent result (and losing 10lb, 4.5kg in weight in the process).

Left: Chess, checkers and backgammon – a 19th century traveling compendium.

Above: A pocket set, useful for working out problems or playing postal chess.

American Grandmaster George Koltanowski specialized in this form of chess and in 1937 he gave a display in Edinburgh against 34 opponents, setting a world record. He won 24 and drew 10. Blindfold chess was discouraged by the Soviets, believing the strain of performing such feats could cause a mental breakdown. Because of this, modern masters have not specialized in blindfold chess to the same extent as in the past, but occasionally an exhibition is organized, proving it is well within their ability.

CHESS CLOCKS

Chess clocks were first introduced in 1883, at the London international tournament won by Zukertort. The clocks had become necessary as some players would play very slowly and take an hour or more on one move. Games could last for over ten hours. The first design was of two pendulum clocks placed on a see-saw stand. By pushing down, one clock would stop, and the other in an upright position would start.

BLINDFOLD CHESS DISPLAYS

Amazingly, chess played without sight of the board has been around since the 9th century, when the Arab chess masters would play a game with their eyes blindfolded. These achievements had been forgotten until Philidor astounded the nobility in the 18th century by playing three blindfold games simultaneously. Since then many masters have cultivated this special skill.

Left: A relaxed Blackburne in 1889 showing his "blindfold" skills against members of a London club.

Below: A novelty timer: you must move before the ball reaches the end.

Above: An early tilting clock.

In the 19th century Morphy, Blackburne and Zukertort expanded upon this remarkable feat by regularly playing eight or more opponents simultaneously. When Paul Morphy played eight games in Birmingham in 1858, the *Illustrated London News* devoted a full page to the event, reporting each game, and included a portrait of Morphy, who won six games, lost one and drew one.

For national and international tournaments the standard time has become 40 moves to be played in two hours, followed by 20 moves for each following hour. If a player fails to make a time control he loses the game. For local chess events the time controls will normally be set at a quicker rate of play. With the modern digital electronic timer, an exciting form of chess is enjoyed, where each player has only five minutes for all his moves. Chess masters and club players love to relax by playing one minute chess, during which time they will often play 70 moves or more. This probably qualifies chess as the fastest game ever played!

TOURNAMENT CHESS

"Tournament" is a word that used to refer only to the medieval jousts arranged between knights on horseback. In 1841 George Walker, founder of the first chess clubs, the Westminster and St. George's in London, wrote in "Bell's Life" about a gathering of Yorkshiremen meeting to play chess. Walker described it as being a "tournament." This term became accepted and was used for the first international chess meeting held in London in 1851.

The World Chess Federation (FIDE) organizes a series of tournaments that theoretically make it possible for anyone to become the next World Champion. All one would have to do is (1) win a national title which qualifies for (2) a Zonal tournament, from which one can qualify for (3) an Interzonal, from which one may qualify to play in (4) the Candidates' Match tournament. Winning this qualifies you to play (5) the World Champion for his title. Easy really, the whole process should take no more than three years!

For keen chess players there are tournaments being played most weekends. They usually start on Friday evening for the first round, three rounds are then played on Saturday and usually two on Sunday. They use a system where winners in one round meet one another in the next round, so for the winners each round becomes progressively harder. The number of entrants is limited to the size of the venue, but everyone is guaranteed a game for each round.

Left: This drawing records an international Ladies Tournament which was held in London in the 19th century.

Speed tournaments have recently become popular. Here the rounds are organized on a knock-out basis. To qualify for the next round, two players first play two games in which they have only 25 minutes to play all their moves. If both games finish in a draw, they must then play two games of five minutes each. If the result is still drawn, then they play a game where White is given six minutes against five minutes for Black. If this game is drawn, Black wins the right to go through to the next round. This is tough on pure chess but brilliant for sheer excitement.

COLLECTORS CHESS

Chess can be enjoyed without playing the game at all. Philately is a hobby of World Chess Champion, Anatoloy Karpov. For collectors there are enough international issues of stamps with a chess theme to form a subject of specialized interest. Related collectables are post-marks, postcards, cigarette cards, and – a recent addition – picture telephone cards. One from Germany for 40 units shows a design incorporating a rook and knight.

Hanon Russell, of Connecticut, has enjoyed decades amassing a large reference source of original letters, photographs, and historical documents related to chess. German Grandmaster Lothar Schmid has a passion for collecting old chess manuscripts and literature, and this has resulted over the years in his accumulating the world's largest private collection of such material.

Chess Collectors International is an umbrella organization for all varieties of chess collectors. Every two years a congress is convened where seminars are held to discuss chess history, culture, and of course collecting. Eminent museums, such as the Victoria and Albert, London, the Metropolitan Museum of Art, New York, and the two foremost museums of Bavaria, in Munich and Nuremberg, have all co-operated during these congresses by organizing public exhibitions of their chess artifacts, chess boards and chess sets. Member's chess set collections have also been displayed at their congress meetings, and at the World Chess Championship matches held in London and New York. Chess is certainly a multi-faceted game, and if this book has encouraged you to take an interest in it, you will find that a whole new world beckons you.

THE ROYAL GAME OF CHESS

" **I**f a ruler does not understand chess, how can he rule over a kingdom".

Sassanian King of Kings, Khusros II, c.600 A.D.

Right: Originally captioned "Check. But how long will the game last?", this cartoon shows English Prime Minister Benjamin Disraeli in 1878 contemplating events in the war with Russia over the disputed territory of Afghanistan. Note that the White queen is Victoria.

Above: The Tsarevich of Russia, playing chess, is seen with other European royalty in Denmark.

CHESS IN LEGEND

One of the earliest legends explains how chess, then known as "chatrang" was brought to Iran from India, in the reign of King Khusrau Nushirwan (531-579). A Rajah of India sent his vizier, escorting a generous tribute of camels and elephants, to the Shah's court. The vizier presented a message on silk which the Rajah of India had sent to Nushirwan. Accompanying it was a games board constructed so carefully and with such art that a treasure-house had been emptied for it. The message which the Indian brought from the Rajah was to this effect:

"May you live as long as the skies endure! Bid those who have been most engaged in pursuit of science to place the games board before you and let each man express his opinion as to how this subtle game is played. Let them identify each piece by name, declare how it must be moved and upon which square. They must be able to identify the foot-soldier, and the movements of the vizier and the shah. If they discover how this subtle game is played, they will have surpassed all other sages and I will gladly send to your court the duty and tribute which you exact. If, on the other hand, the council of notable men of Iran fail utterly in this science and prove themselves to be unequal with us in it, you will no longer be able to exact from this land and territory of ours any kind of tribute or duty. You, on the other hand, will submit to the payment of tribute; for science is superior to any wealth however noteworthy."

The sages of Nushirwan were baffled, except for the greatest of them all, Bozorgmehr. After two days' study he described how the game was played.

"The sage has invented a battlefield, in the midst of which the king takes up his station. To left and right of him the army is dispersed, the foot soldiers occupying the rank in front. At the king's side stands his sagacious counsellor advising him on the strategy to be carried out during the battle. In two directions the elephants are posted with their faces turned toward where the conflict is. Beyond them are stationed the war-horses, on which are mounted two resourceful riders, and fighting alongside them on either hand to right and left are the chariots ready for the fray."

The Indian envoy conceded to Bozorgmehr, and the Rajah paid double tribute and duties to Khusrau Nushirwan.

Above: "A New Game of Chess *not* to be found in Philidor," the cartoon satirizes relations between King George IV and Parliament at a time when political emancipation for Catholics in Great Britain was a burning issue of the day.

ROYAL APPROVAL

Since these early times chess has been popular with ruling dynasties. The Arabian caliphs adopted the game with enthusiasm from the Persians. Many became good players and enjoyed games against their own "grandees," professional players maintained at the Arabian courts. A debate (that is still continuing today) concerned whether chess is an acceptable activity in accordance with the laws of the Koran. Caliph Walid II (12th century), aware of the dispute, was playing chess when an unexpected courier arrived from Sicily. The Caliph ordered his servant to cover the board with a cloth. He then questioned the visitor on his knowledge of the Koran, and realizing the man was ignorant about Muslim religion, Caliph Walid uncovered the chessboard and continued playing with the remark "there is nothing forbidden to the unlearned."

At this time chess spread through Europe, via the Moors in Spain and Christian knights returning from the Crusades. England's Danish King Canute (c.995-1035) supposedly donated his crystal chess set to Hyde Abbey, Winchester. Another legend concerns King Canute playing chess with his kinsman, the Earl

of Ulf. The King left a knight "en prise" and Ulf took it. The King asked if he could take his last move back; Ulf refused, upset the board and walked away. Canute was furious, and called him a coward. Ulf reminded the King that he had not been a coward when he had saved them in a battle against the Swedes. The next day, Canute, still furious, ordered his bodyguard, Ivor the White, to kill the Earl, even though he knew that Ulf had gone to sleep in St. Luke's Church for sanctuary.

A LOVE MATCH

King Edward III used a game of chess to try to seduce Princess Joan of Wales, the Countess of Salisbury, who was reputed to be the most beautiful and dazzling woman in Britain. The stake of the game was the lady's honor. However, the Countess had the courage to defeat the King, checkmating him with her bishop. The Countess then offered the King the services of one of her damsels. The King politely refused, and rode off with his knights. This game was supposedly played at Warwick Castle in 1341, at which time the Earl of Salisbury was a prisoner in France.

Chess became very important to the feudal lords during the Middle Ages. It was a necessary skill for young squires to obtain during their apprenticeship to knighthood. It was also prevalent among the clerics, who were normally from the ranks of the gentry, providing them with some relaxation from the discipline of monastic life. Rooks and checkered boards were often incorporated into a family's heraldic coat of arms. The English squire, John Walcot of Walcote, had a rook included into his coat of arms in a memorable way. Playing a game of chess with Henry V after the battle of Agincourt, Squire Walcote checkmated the King with a rook. The King immediately honored him for his courage, and awarded him a rook, henceforth to be placed on his heraldic shield.

RUSSIAN RULERS

In Russia the Tsars loved their chess. The game became, by order, the favorite pastime of the Russian Court. Ivan the Terrible died while in the middle of a game. Peter the Great played chess during his war campaigns and encouraged the play of chess among the nobility. Catherine the Great enjoyed playing chess with Prince Potyomkin Tavrichesky, of whom it was said "With one hand he is playing chess, with the other he is conquering the people."

Rome's ambassador to Moscow in 1670-73, reporting on the children of the Tsar, wrote, "The Russians do not at all permit dancing, fist fights, and other noble exercises that are widespread among us. They play so-called chess, the famous Persian game, a truly royal game by its name and nature. They play daily, and they develop their intellect with it to a surprising degree."

Above: Entitled "Political checkmate": here we see international intrigue in 1829 when the Russian Tsar tried to gain control over Turkish territory.

Below: In 1814, financed by Britain's John Bull (holding the globe), the Allies plan to checkmate Napoleon's plans to dominate Europe. Waterloo was a year away.

Emperor Napoleon Bonaparte was an avid chess player, having played at the famous Café de la Régence in Paris when a young officer. He retained a passion for the game throughout his life. When a prisoner at St. Helena he was presented with a magnificent carved Chinese ivory chess set, marked with eagles, and the initial "N" surmounted by the imperial crown. The presenter of the set was the brother of an English officer, who gave it as a gesture of thanks to the Emperor for taking his brother prisoner, thereby saving his life when he was wounded. This incident took place during a skirmish at Quatre Bras, a campaign leading up to the battle of Waterloo.

AMERICAN ADVENTURES

The United States might still be a colony of England if it had not been for the game of chess that Colonel Johann Rall was playing the evening before the Battle of Trenton (December 26, 1776). An English sympathizer sent his son with a note warning the general that Washington was planning to cross the Delaware and attack. Colonel Rall, engrossed in his game, carelessly pocketed the note. After the battle, the colonel was found mortally wounded, the note still in his pocket, unread. The Battle of Trenton is regarded by many historians as a turning point in the American War of Independence. Before Trenton the British were successful; after Trenton, it was the colonists who obtained success. The United States of America, born because a Hessian soldier was addicted to chess!

George Washington enjoyed an occasional game of chess. His Red v. White English ivory chess set has survived and is kept at the U.S. National Museum.

Below: An English 18th century set similar in style to one owned by George Washington.

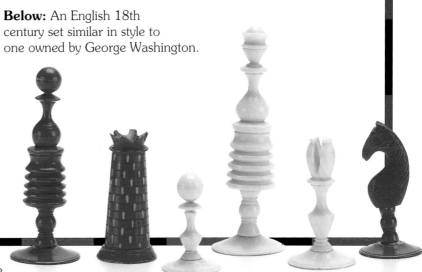

Two other distinguished leaders of the new American States also appreciated their chess, Benjamin Franklin and Thomas Jefferson. They both collected contemporary chess literature and owned a number of chess sets with boards. Some of these have survived, including a carved ivory set obtained by Jefferson when he was American Minister in Paris.

ENGLISH ENTHUSIASTS

English monarchs have enjoyed a long association with chess since William the Conqueror and his Normans brought the game with them to England in 1066 and entrenched it into British culture. The earliest chessmen in Britain were found during an archaeological excavation at the site of Loughor Norman castle, South Wales. These simple chess pieces are carved out of antler and date from the 11th century.

Above: Henry VIII had more chess sets than wives!

A description of Edward I (1239-1307) states that he was the master of legal argument, formidable at arms and excelled at chess. There is also an account that he owned a jasper and crystal chess set with a

board. Another monarch, Henry VIII (1491-1547) famous for his six wives, also had a collection of at least eleven chess sets. Most of them were carved out of bone, and kept in satin bags or black leather boxes.

Above: Elizabeth I played chess avidly.

Henry's renowned daughter, Elizabeth I (1533-1603), learned chess from her tutor Roger Ascham, and enjoyed it as one of her favored recreations. Elizabeth, when attending a jousting tournament, presented Sir Charles Blount with a "Queen at Chess of gold richly enamelled" for distinguishing himself at tilting. He tied it onto his arm with a crimson ribbon, as a token of her favor.

A play by Thomas Middleton, "*A Game at Chess*" was presented at the Globe Theatre in London in 1624. The play was written at a time when the people of England were celebrating the news of the collapse of negotiations for Prince Charles's Spanish marriage. A satire, using the game of chess as its vehicle, it poured scorn on Catholics in general and Gondemar, the Spanish Ambassador, in particular. It was so popular that it was necessary to be at the theater two hours before the start in order to obtain admission. The receipts for nine performances amounted to £1,500, a record for those times. At the Spanish Ambassador's protest, the play was closed down, and the players summoned before the Privy Council. Thomas Middleton actually spent a short period in prison as a result.

King Charles 1 (1600-49) was also fond of playing chess. The Countess of Warwick recollected that "the King when he is neither in the field, nor at the Council, passes most of his time at chess with the Marquis of Winchester." Charles was playing chess when a messenger arrived with the news that his Scottish army had surrendered to Parliament Forces under Cromwell in 1647. Charles was the only British king to be beheaded (not allowed in chess). In 1649 there was a sale of his effects, and included was a chess board described as being inlaid with gold, silver and pearls. Originally it had been the property of Queen Elizabeth; it was sold for £23.

Queen Victoria and Prince Albert also enjoyed playing chess. Prince Albert believing it to be good for the mind, saw to it that their children were all taught the game. A set Prince Albert had as a boy in Germany is now kept at the London Museum, while another carved terracotta chess set of theirs can be seen at the Victoria and Albert Museum.

The present British Royal family continue their traditional interest in chess. Princess Diana attended the 1993 World Chess Championship match, held in London, between Nigel Short and Garry Kasparov, while in the national press it was reported that Prince William, when visiting a refuge for the homeless with his mother, enjoyed playing chess with one of the men staying there.

Above: Charles I, another keen chess monarch.

Left: In 1837 a young Queen Victoria has to be careful of the moves of Lord Palmerston, the Foreign Secretary. Her Prime Minister, Lord Melbourne, keeps a watchful eye over their game.